AN AMERICAN GIRL IN INDIA

ALSO BY WENDY DONIGER IN SPEAKING TIGER

The Hindus: An Alternative History

Reading the Kamasutra: *The Mare's Trap and Other Essays on Vatsyayana's Masterpiece*

The Ring of Truth: Myths of Sex and Jewelry

Beyond Dharma: Dissent in the Ancient Indian Sciences of Sex And Politics

Winged Stallions and Wicked Mares: Horses in Indian Myth and History

The Dream Narrative: The Dreams of God and Mortals in Classical Hinduism

AN AMERICAN GIRL IN INDIA

Letters and Recollections, 1963–64

Wendy Doniger

SPEAKING
TIGER

SPEAKING TIGER BOOKS LLP
125A, Ground Floor, Shahpur Jat, near Asiad Village,
New Delhi 110049

First published by Speaking Tiger Books 2022

Copyright © Wendy Doniger 2022

ISBN: 978-93-5447-285-5
eISBN: 978-93-5447-286-2

10 9 8 7 6 5 4 3 2 1

Typeset in Crimson Text by SÜRYA, New Delhi
Printed at Chaman Enterprises, New Delhi

For my students, who were also young in India,
and for Ravi Singh, whose courage, loyalty,
and literary finesse never failed me

Contents

Preface

In August of 1963, when I was twenty-two, just one year past my graduation from Radcliffe College, I landed in what was then called Calcutta (now called Kolkata) on my first trip to India. I had a year's grant to study Sanskrit and Bangla (which we then called Bengali), the language of Bengal.

Fast forward. In January of 2019, when I was seventy-eight and had just retired after forty years of teaching at the University of Chicago, I was clearing out my office in the Divinity School and came upon a box of letters tucked away behind a cabinet. I opened one of the letters and read, 'Calcutta, December 10, 1963. Dear Mommy and Daddy, ...' These letters, typed on the trusty little Hermes typewriter that I carried with me everywhere in those days, had apparently been saved by my mother and must have come back to me on the tidal wave of books and papers that overwhelmed me when she died in 1991. Now, in my

office, almost thirty years after I received them, and almost
sixty years after I had written them, I opened the box.

This book is an annotated edition of those parts of
these thirty-three long letters that discuss my experiences
in and thoughts about India at that time.

Where I Was

My Harvard professor and mentor, Daniel H.H. Ingalls, had
very old-fashioned ideas about women (and much else) and
was concerned for my safety during my year abroad. So he
arranged for me to live in Shantiniketan ('Abode of Peace'),
a school situated in the countryside near the tiny village
of Bolpur in the district of Birbhum in what became, after
Partition, West Bengal, some 95 miles (or 152 kilometres)
north of Calcutta. Rabindranath Tagore had settled there
in 1901 on land that his father, Debendranath Tagore,
had bought in 1863. In 1951, Shantiniketan had become
a university, Visva-Bharati ('All India'), largely dedicated
to the arts, music, literature, painting, and theatre, and
in particular to the poetry and music and philosophy of
Tagore. By 1963, it had become in part a finishing school
for upper-class Bengali girls, and Ingalls thought I would
be safe and happy there. And, as usual, he was right. I lived
in room 16 of Birla Hostel of the Vidya Bhavan ('Scholars'
Block', the Humanities branch of the University), named
after the wealthy Birla family that had endowed the building
and inhabited by women from all over India and abroad.

Eventually I left Shantiniketan to live in Calcutta, where
I stayed in the home of Edward Cameron Dimock and his
wife Lorraine and five children. (With the serendipity that

was to halo me throughout my time in India, I just happened to meet the Dimock family on my flight from London to Calcutta [see the letter of August 15, 1963].) Dimock, a professor of Bengali at the University of Chicago, was the Director of the American Institute of Indian Studies, which had funded my year in India. The Dimock family apartment, at 12/2 Swinhoe Street, Calcutta – 19 (the section known as Ballygunge, in south Calcutta), was also the headquarters of the AIIS. Years later, in 1978, I joined Dimock at the University of Chicago, where he headed the Department of South Asian Languages and Civilizations and I became a Professor myself. He retired in 1993 and moved to Cape Cod, where I too had a summer house, and we met there often, until his death in 2001.

There is one story about Ed Dimock that he told me, during the Chicago years, long after we had both left Calcutta, a story that I've always loved and that tells a great deal about the sort of man he was, though he always used to tell it as a parable about the importance of learning foreign languages well. It seems that on one of their trips to India, at the end of the long series of flights from Chicago to Calcutta (changing at Reykjavik, Frankfurt, Beirut, etc.), the Dimocks (Ed, Lorraine, and five children under the age of ten) finally made their way to the Swinhoe Street house in the middle of the night. The house was locked, in total darkness, and there was no one there to let them in. The five children had wet themselves, soiled themselves, thrown up on themselves, and were now bawling with exhaustion. Ed finally managed to rouse the chowkidar (janitor/doorman), and when the man arrived Ed simply lost it, and let loose with a string of Bengali invectives, telling him what he thought of him, of his mother, of his sister, of his relationship with his sister, and on and on, all in fluent Bengali. Finally he ran out of breath and immediately regretted his outburst; the chowkidar was, after all, not the problem, and Ed, a kindly soul and a Unitarian minister to boot, was truly sorry that he had offended an innocent man. But before he could catch his breath to apologize, the chowkidar said, 'Sir, how well you speak Bengali!' (*Shaheb, ki bhaalo Bangla bolte paaren!*)

I myself had an adventure in India that similarly proved the advantages of linguistic training, an event that I failed to report in my letters. When I was in Benares I stayed at Clark's Hotel, the big old colonial hotel, which apparently branded me as a certain sort of tourist. And so, whenever I left the hotel, I was mobbed by men trying to sell me all sorts of tourist junk I didn't want, and when I went to the shops that sold paintings, they showed me only the badly executed modern copies of the old paintings. On one occasion, I happened to turn the picture over and read the Sanskrit inscription out loud and translated it. 'Oh!' said the shopkeeper. 'You know *Sanskrit!*' And immediately he ordered tea to be brought for me and also brought out the folders with the genuine old paintings.

There is also a great story about Lorraine Dimock that somehow never found its way into my letters. Ed was in the habit of inviting home to dinner anyone that he became interested in, and Lorraine had to feed them, on what were always fairly short rations which became, during the years building up to the India–Pakistan War of 1965, very short rations indeed. One day Ed announced that he had invited a Hindu, a Muslim, a Jew, and a Catholic to dinner (it does sound like the beginning of a joke), and Lorraine had to produce a meal without offending any of them. She invited them for a Friday and served pork, which was equally taboo to all of them (the Hindu a vegetarian, the Jew and Muslim forbidden to eat pig, and the Catholic still observing the meatless Friday rule). No one was offended, as all were equally offended, and they all ate everything.

From Calcutta I travelled, usually with women friends I had met at Shantiniketan or in Calcutta, sometimes alone, later with my mother, to other parts of India, down to what was then Madras and Madurai and Mahabalipuram, to Bombay and Ajanta, through Rajasthan, to Khajuraho and Udaipur and Benares, back east to Puri and Bhubaneshwar, and up to Kathmandu. Everywhere I went, I wrote letters to my parents, except when my mother was travelling with me.

Who I Was

The letters constitute a rather peculiar lens through which to view my impressions of India at that time. They are not private, like a diary, nor, at the other extreme, were they intended for publication. They are a mixed genre, part intimate, introspective letters to my parents and part field notes, long, highly detailed passages of description and meditation which were designed ultimately to be used in the writing of my PhD dissertation. They already contain the seeds of many of the interests that would carry me through the writing of my books over the next half century. The author of these letters is already mad about Shiva (the hero of my first book, *Siva: The Erotic Ascetic*, 1973), fascinated by the wickedness of the gods (*The Origins of Evil in Hindu Mythology*, 1976), intrigued by the wife of the Sun, who turns into a mare to flee from her husband and children (*Winged Stallions and Wicked Mares*, 2021), and so forth.

But the tone of much of the letters, framing those more public passages, is extremely personal and reveals how extraordinarily close I was to my parents, whom I still called, after all, 'Mommy and Daddy'. Indeed, many years later, long after both of them had died, I wrote a book about them and about my relationship with them.[*] One stunning piece of evidence of that intimacy, in the letters, is the fact that they planned to visit me in India. My father had to cancel his trip at the last minute, to deal with a crisis in his publishing company (he published *Pulpit Digest*, a magazine for the Protestant clergy[†]). But my mother made the trip. This now seems to me quite extraordinary. How many scholars do I know who brought their parents along on research trips? And how many parents would go to the trouble of travelling to India to visit their daughter there? And so the letters contain pages and pages of banausic details about the planning of the parental visit and its scheduling, as well as pages asking them to send me this and that and asking them if they had received that and this that I had sent to them, and about how much I appreciated

---

* *The Donigers of Great Neck: A Mythologized Memoir.*

† See *The Donigers of Great Neck.*

their letters. I left all of that out of this book. But I left in some now embarrassing remarks meant only for the eyes of doting parents, such as 'Everyone is terribly impressed with my Sanskrit and my burgeoning Bengali!' (August 15, 1963)

I also edited out a lot about my impending marriage. I had married at the end of my junior year at Radcliffe, in large part in order to get out of the dormitory, which I loathed. The marriage lasted less than a year; I was divorced at twenty-one. But I never mentioned this to anyone in India, and so I was truly surprised when my friend Chanchal guessed it, ostensibly from reading my palm (September 27, 1963). Now I was planning to marry

With my husband in my white, gold-encrusted Benarsi sari, in my home on our wedding day, March 31, 1964.

again, as soon as I returned from India, and I did, on March 31, 1964. I left all of that out of this book. But I couldn't resist including, after describing how Parvati's parents thought that Shiva wasn't good enough for her, a brief remark about 'the way that parents are about daughters, even if they marry gods', a not-so-oblique reference to my own forthcoming marriage (August 28, 1963), and another aside about 'the attitude of fathers towards sons-in-law' (October 9, 1963).

Though I didn't tell my parents how much I missed my fiancé while I was in India, I told Chanchal, and so she taught me to knit, and I spent many hours under Chanchal's tutelage knitting a sweater for him. The more I missed him, the larger he grew in my imagination, and I made the sweater bigger and bigger, so that when I finally returned home and gave it to him it was hilariously enormous, and we called it the 'monster' and used it as a blanket.

Finally, I cut many, but not all, passages telling my parents how homesick I was. I didn't tell them how I cried into my pillow every night at the Ramakrishna Mission in Calcutta, and, when the pillow became hot and wet, turned it over to cry into the other side. But references to my homesickness kept leaking into discussions of other topics, particularly when I tried to analyse my state of mind as I lived in India, and I have kept those passages in this book. Even the descriptive passages about India constantly reveal my deep intimacy with the two people I was telling all of this to, my assumption that we all knew the same jokes and have read the same books and have lived in the same places and, indeed, feel the same about the most important human matters. I shared with my parents so much of the literature and art and music and jokes of several cultures, particularly Viennese and New York Jewish culture, that on many occasions when I resorted, in a letter, to a familiar analogy to try to explain to my parents something uniquely Indian, I had to add footnotes to this book to let the reader, particularly but not only the Indian reader, in on the joke or the literary allusion. These many references to the world of my home were like so many lifelines that

I threw out for myself when I was so overwhelmed by the foreignness of so many of my experiences in India that I could only make sense of them, especially at the start, by comparing them to some roughly parallel phenomenon in a book, or painting, or opera, or song, or saying that I knew from my familiar childhood world. And an aura of childhood hovers over even the literary citations, which do include references to Pascal and Pindar but begin with *Peter Pan* and end with *Winnie-the-Pooh* and cite a number of other children's books along the way, most frequently Lewis Carroll's *Alice's Adventures in Wonderland* and *Through the Looking Glass*, my favourite books.

On the other hand, precisely because the letters were directed to my parents, they were in some ways highly censored right from the start, a reverse twist on Parental Guidance. Not to put too fine a point on it, I either left out or lied outright about a number of my experiences in India. (Had this actually been a diary, I would surely have included a lot of sensational incidents, recalling what Gwendolen Fairfax says in Oscar Wilde's *The Importance of Being Earnest*: 'I never travel without my diary. One should always have something sensational to read in the train.') One does not tell one's parents the truth about danger or disgrace, or at least I did not. For example, I never told them how very ill I was in India, how I suffered from both amoebic and bacillary dysentery; my illness finally made me leave India several months earlier than I had intended, by which time the local doctors were treating my condition with arsenic, and I continued to be ill for several years after my return from India. (I vividly remember how I kept trotting back and forth every week or two from my apartment in Cambridge to the Harvard Health Center, through Harvard Yard, carrying one of those little white paper boxes with metal handles that we used to carry home leftovers from Chinese restaurants, but these contained my stool samples.) Yet a casual reference (on September 15, 1963) to sulfaguanidine and enterovioform, drugs used in the treatment of dysentery, suggests that I must have told my parents *something* about my health problem, despite the fact that I kept insisting how healthy I was, 'protest[ing] too much, methinks'.

I have therefore added, in this preface and in the introductions to the several parts into which I've divided my letters, some of the lurid details that I left out of the letters in order not to shock my parents but that I still vividly recall, precisely because they were so shocking to me, too, at that time.

I didn't tell my parents how totally stoned Ed Dimock and I became from drinking several glasses of *bhang lassi* (a sweet milky drink made from liquid marijuana) on the night of Durga Puja (October 28, 1963). As it was my first experience of *bhang lassi*, I mistook it for a delicious milkshake, downed the first one in just a few swallows, and cheerfully asked for a second one, wondering only in retrospect why everyone giggled at my request. Ed, of course, knew what he was doing. We then drove out in the jeep, with the rest of the family, along the Calcutta Maidan, a big circular park that was dark at night. Ed was so high that he thought that he was in Chicago and that the Maidan was Lake Michigan, and he wanted to jump out of the jeep to go and swim in the Lake. It took all of us to restrain him. My notes on the ceremony that we attended that night are rather sketchy, as, thanks to the *bhang lassi*, I had only a rather hazy memory of a lot of lights and noise.

Nor did I tell my parents how I often spent the night before a dawn train departure sleeping on the floor in the Third Class Ladies' Waiting Room at the station. (We wrapped our money and tickets in a sari that we used for a pillow, and there was a chowkidar who watched over us all.) I often travelled alone in those days, and never worried about my personal safety. I was, perhaps, young and foolish, or lucky, or just instinctively limiting my travels to places where I was safe.

Another story that I censored from my parents was the occasion of my first attendance at the sacrifice of a goat. I described the sacrifice in all of its gory detail (October 28, 1963), but then merely noted, 'I decided I wanted a breath of fresh air.' 'Wanted a breath of fresh air' is a wee bit of an understatement. As soon as the head of the goat sprang free from the body, I passed out cold right there in the family temple, and my friends had to carry me out into the fresh air and give me water and fan me until I came to, therefore missing the rest of the ceremony (as of course I did too). And that put an end to any ideas I had had about becoming an anthropologist; I decided to stick to Sanskrit texts.

More seriously, I did not mention to my parents that I was experiencing the first skirmishes of what eventually became the India–Pakistan War of 1965. In Calcutta, right in my own neighbourhood of Ballygunge, I saw Muslims attacked and killed by gangs of Hindu boys, and my planned trip to Kashmir was cancelled when the border was closed, never to open again. Worried that my parents would read about these incidents in the newspaper and worry about me, at the height of the violent demonstrations I wrote what I hoped was a reassuring letter (August 28, 1963) and managed to get to the post office to send them a telegram, telling them not to believe what they read in the papers, that it was really all very peaceful in Calcutta, etc. After I sent the telegram, I started home but was immediately overwhelmed by an angry mob and could not get past them to get back to the Dimock house. Suddenly the crowd parted, as a jeep, blowing its horn constantly, inched forward towards me, and there were Ed Dimock and the driver come to get me. I got in and they took me home. I don't think I was ever so glad to see anyone in my life as I was to see that jeep.

Who I Am Now, Reading These Letters

But I did a very different sort of editing of the letters, now, for this book. I was tempted to edit out a number of passages that I found deeply embarrassing. Prime among these are my reactions to Indian poverty, which betray a breathtaking naïvete (beginning in the letter of August 15, 1963) and reveal the spoiled brat I was at the time, truly a Jewish American princess. The letters are peppered with revealing references to things like vacations in Jamaica (where, in the 1950s we used to winter in Ocho Rios, at that time a small undeveloped village over the hills from Kingston) and summer houses on Shelter Island (a small island off the coast of Long Island where we had a house for several summers) and days at Jones Beach (a large public Atlantic Ocean beach on Long Island that we frequented) and weekends at Montauk Manor (a fancy hotel on the very tip of Long Island) and lunches at the Overseas Press Club and auctions at Parke-Bernet—casual remarks that betray my privileged background. (There is a whole constellation of these associations in my reactions to the movie *Sabrina*, in the letter of November 1, 1963.) I also foolishly took it for granted that the people in my narrow circle were representative of all Americans. I admired Indians for 'things that most Americans have not yet come to value' (August 17, 1963), not realizing that many Americans did indeed share those values, though not the Americans I knew. And when I managed, with the help of a friend, to pay for extra food to supplement the basic rations in Shantiniketan (August 17, 1963; a tale surely intended to reassure my parents), I was, to my eternal shame, acting like a proper Memsahib, though I would have protested vehemently had someone pointed this out to me.

On my frequent trips to Manhattan from my home in Great Neck, on the North Shore of Long Island, I would go to the museums or the opera or my ballet classes and then back home again; I never saw the slums of the Lower East Side or Harlem. I therefore suffered from a double culture shock when I experienced the Calcutta slums, still crowded with refugees from Partition: India, and poverty. And I was painfully aware of the gap between my world and theirs: 'I saw a bullock cart loaded with blankets and chairs, carrying someone's entire belongings to a new house. I wonder how many bullock carts it would take for us to move' (September 18, 1963). But I decided not to censor these troubled, ambivalent passages in this book, as they are more naïve and misguided than shameless, revealing a compassionate, if over-sheltered, heart.

Other passages now make me blush for their Orientalism: I loved the old and hated the new in India, just as the British did. The Orientalism/antiquarianism culminates in an eruption of adolescent monomania, in which I express my horror that the world is going to hell and my conviction that I am one of the happy few left to preserve the great old things (December 5, 1963). But I did come to a more balanced view in one of the last letters (February 16, 1964), praising a modern architectural project in Madras that made use of classical Indian forms. I kept these passages in because they had an important consequence: my Orientalism was a taste that eventually led me to use, in my future work, my Sanskrit (but not my Bangla), writing about ancient rather than contemporary India. Other embarrassing remarks also show how scholarly thinking about India (about race, and gender, and colonialism, and so much else), including my own thinking as chronicled in my books, has changed in the past half century. And so I left in all of those passages, too. But I was often tempted to insert, at the beginning of this book, a statement that 'The management does not necessarily share the opinions expressed in this text'.

I corrected typos but not what one of my students once called 'thinkos', errors in thinking, wrong ideas. I corrected punctuation errors and I standardized the spelling of proper names. For this Indian edition, we used Indian/British spellings where I had used the American forms. I left the archaic place names as they were (Calcutta, Benares), but I updated some of the terminology. I generally changed 'Oriental' to 'Indian', 'Mogul' to 'Mughal,' 'Western' to 'American' or 'non-Indian', and 'Negroes' to 'Blacks'. I glossed obscure references in bracketed notes in the text or, for longer notes, in a footnote. Where errors of fact occur, I left them in and supplied a corrective footnote. The sexist language was too pervasive to correct; the reader must just bear with it as an archaism.

What emerges from these letters is the voice of the person I was then, an American girl who embraced Indian excess of all kinds, the bright colours of the women's clothes, the subtle spices of the food (and how I loved eating with my fingers! I'd always hated knives and forks), who loved Indian art that packed so many things into paintings and sculptures that it made Rococo look like Bauhaus. And Indian music, where you slip up the scale instead of having separate notes—everything about India appealed to my personality. The word 'wonderful' recurs again and again and again in these letters (my computer counted forty-seven occurrences); I was truly full of wonder so often that I ran out of other words. Yet, throughout my stay in India, I ricocheted between my deep love of Indian culture and my childish recoiling from the poverty and the suffering. I was haunted by my inability to love everything about India.

What I see and hear in these writings by my young self is a stunning experience of kindness and generosity from a number of complete strangers, as well as lasting friendships with several extraordinary people. I think these magical cross-cultural encounters were made possible in part by my own youth and my great passion for the land of India and its culture, and in part by the youth of the country itself, so newly freed from the colonial yoke, not yet darkened by the rise of a jingoistic and repressive Hindu theocracy. Sadly, I cannot imagine such open-hearted and joyous encounters between an American visitor and the average citizen of the India of today. And yet the memory of those happy and innocent days in India long ago gives me courage to hope.

Part One

PRELUDE IN ENGLAND

The letters begin with one written from London, where I stayed with Ernst and Ilse Gombrich en route to India. Their son Richard was then and remains one of my closest friends. Our discussion about translation foreshadowed, in my letters from India, my several ruminations on Indian metaphors and clichés. I then visited Max Fry (Edwin Maxwell Fry, a modernist architect) and his wife, the architect Jane Drew, friends of a friend of my mother. They had worked for three years with Le Corbusier to create the new capital city of Punjab at Chandigarh. This was my first, but not my last, encounter with British colonial attitudes to India.

Not surprisingly, the pervasive theme of homesickness begins even in the records of my very first days in India, in fact on my flight from London to Calcutta. One of the ways I dealt with the strangeness of it all was to fantasize meeting old friends from home; hence the reference to Stephen Albert, a Great Neck High School friend who went on to win the 1985 Pulitzer Prize for Music for his Symphony No. 1 *RiverRun*, and died in 1992 in an ice storm in Truro, on Cape Cod (not far from my own summer house there); and to Daisy Schott, one of my mother's many Viennese cousins. This fantasy of encountering familiar faces in the strange land was realized early in my stay in Calcutta (August 15, 1963), when I met a boy I had known through another Great Neck High School friend, Mickey Solomon.

I am at a loss to explain the fact that the first letter contains one of only two short references to Nabaneeta Dev Sen in this entire correspondence. I saw Nabaneeta often when I was in Calcutta, but for some reason she never again—after August 15, 1963 (in Part II)—made her way into the extant letters to my parents. Nabaneeta and her husband Amartya Sen had been among my closest friends at Harvard during the previous year, when both Amartya and Richard Gombrich had been Harkness Fellows, and Nabaneeta and I had read Sanskrit texts with Professor Ingalls. Nabaneeta and I remained friends all of her life; after her death, I spoke at her memorial in 2021. Amartya and I have stayed in touch throughout the years.

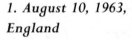

1. August 10, 1963,
England

[Stopping at Stratford:] At night we went down to the river, and during the intermission of the play, too, and watched the flocks of swans floating down, asleep, head under wing, gliding in and out of the darkness like so many moons weaving through clouds. Silent and ancient.

[From a conversation with Ernst Gombrich:] We have lovely talks over breakfast about the theory of perception and the translation of clichés: Is it being false to the tone of the original to translate literally, and therefore often strikingly, a figure of speech which has become so trite as to be a nonentity in the original? Answer: Since you have lost so much of the author's original beauty in translating, you owe him a little something, and can repay this debt in part by allowing the cliché to become striking in translation.

A false note was struck in the midst of all this euphoria. I went to see Max Fry and Jane Drew. I asked her, 'Well, what do you do when you get sick in India?' and she said, 'You go to England,' and I said, 'Well, what do the Indians do?' and she said, 'The wealthy Indians go to England.'

[I had a] letter from Nabaneeta [Dev Sen] saying that she will be in Calcutta on the 13th and will come to meet me if I call her from the airport.

2. August 13, 1963, 2nd Star to the Left*

I'm writing this from the plane [from London to Calcutta] but will post it the minute I reach the Land of the Gods so that you will know I arrived safely. As for my post-arrival adventures, they must be written on my forehead, as the Hindus believe all fate to be, but I'm afraid my linguistic talents don't extend to that sphere.

Small world department. I am seated in this plane next to an Indian man with eyes like an ibis or perhaps a unicorn; I found out, in the course of a delightful conversation, (a) that he works as an ad man on Madison Avenue, and (b) that he is the first cousin of Khurshed Sahiar, the Parsi doctor who visited us on New Year's 1962. I just know that when I get to Calcutta someone will approach me playing the sitar and begging and it will be Stevie Albert or Daisy Schott. I will have to disguise myself.

---

* These are the directions that Peter Pan gives for the way to reach Never Never Land. This letter was handwritten.

The Air India flight stops at Paris, Frankfurt, Beirut, Bombay, and Calcutta, *not*, as one might expect upon a moment's consideration, in Karachi. The India–Pakistan spite is so bitter that Indian time is ten minutes ahead of West Pakistan time, ten minutes behind East Pakistan time, just to make everything difficult. Travelling on Air India is pleasant and easy; there is never any doubt as to where to go [in airports] for the plane or customs or the restaurant—you just follow the line of saris.

As I landed and all the excitement of being in India came over me, I was strongly conscious of the feeling that I was landing in a country that really belonged to the Indians, and was not just a playground for Europeans. The Indian pilot and stewardesses left, and the Indian officials checked me through. (No import duties on anything, because they were so happy that I am going to Shantiniketan: there should have been a tremendous duty on the camera, but the official winked at me and said he would write that it was over five years old.) There were very few white people in the streets, even though the architecture and signs were very English.

Part Two

ARRIVAL AND FIRST DAYS
IN INDIA

When I first arrived in India, I went straight to the Ramakrishna Mission in south Calcutta, where American students often stayed while looking for more permanent lodgings. Even there I was still reminded of home, as when I met an American girl who, like me, planned to be married the day she got off the plane from India, and when men musselling in a lake in Calcutta reminded me of clamming on Shelter Island, where we used to stand knee-deep or waist-deep in the water to fish for clams with our toes. On several occasions, small children reminded me of my little brother Tony, who was twelve years old when I went to India. At this stage of my time in India, I was still stunningly naïve about the country, assuming that Indian children never begged, but also already trying to deal with the problem of caste, as in my first encounters with people socially relegated to the 'lowest' professions, people that I called (parroting what I heard) 'sweepers' or 'outcastes', now called Dalits, formerly called Untouchables.

❧

3. August 15, 1963,
Ramakrishna Mission, Calcutta

I have just discovered that if you don't actually watch the postman cancel the stamp on your letter, he takes it off and throws out the letter, so now I don't know whether you received the letter I sent from the airport. I hope you did. Well, anyway, you'll get this one. If you ever have any important letters, or especially long ones, or, especially, letters with enclosures such as photographs, please register them. It doesn't cost much more, at least not at this end, and it saves much heartache.

I have much to tell you about Calcutta. But I have discovered at least one important thing about myself: I don't have fun doing things alone. The first day I knew no one and went by myself and was terribly homesick. The second day (I had to stay in Calcutta an extra day because I arrived just in time for Independence Day with everything closed, so I had to wait for a banking day before going to Shantiniketan), I was with an American girl on a Fulbright and a Sikh systems analyst, and I had a marvellous time and am completely cured of my homesickness.

New instalments of Small World. On the plane, after I had finished my letter to you, I met a man from the Midwest, obviously a teacher, who was having quite a time travelling with his wife and five children. I expressed my sympathy, and we got to talking, and he turned out to be Ed Dimock, travelling to India for the third time, the author of the book of Bengali tales, *The Thief of Love*, and Ingalls's pupil and [the man Ingalls had intended to be] my Calcutta mentor. So he took me under his wing, and the people who met him in Calcutta took me home with them

too, and gave me all the low down, and sent me here to the
Ramakrishna Mission, which is air conditioned and clean
and full of scholars and all sorts of wonderful people. And
when I sat down to dinner here, I looked across the table
straight into the eyes of a boy I met years ago at Mickey
Solomon's house. And next to me was a girl on a Fulbright
who is planning to be married the day she gets off the plane
next June. And sitting next to her was a lovely Hindu who
just kept saying, as we gushed over each other, 'People are
the same all over.'

The heat is not bad at all. It is very humid, but one
soon gets used to being wet all through, and I don't even
carry an umbrella; the monsoon is not too heavy here,
and when it rains and you're outside you just get rained
on. Everyone else is wet through too, so you don't even
bother to mop your brow.

The people do live in the street, but they are dressed
in clean saris and dhotis, washing and shaving and telling
jokes, and I guess I subconsciously feel that when the man
lying down on the sidewalk wakes up, he will get up and
walk home. At any rate, it is not as pitiful as one might
expect; to an American it looks more like fun than like the
squalor of American slums. The streets have a strong smell
of sweat and urine, but a very strange flavour of urine;
and I was quite surprised to notice, when I went to the
bathroom tonight, that my urine is beginning to smell that
way too. The children in the street are all very beautiful,
neatly and cleanly dressed, and they don't beg. They are
completely spoiled by their parents, who manage to deny
them nothing, no matter how dire their poverty.

I am assured by those who should know that there

are no poisonous snakes at Shantiniketan, and no malaria anywhere in the North. I am taking very good care of my health, but I am not squeamish. There are great big lizards here, much larger than the ones in South America, and everyone loves them and I do too.

There are also many Midwestern Americans, teachers and girls on Fulbrights and men doing research; and one very nice boy who is working on a marvellous surrealistic painting of the temptation of Saint Anthony explained to me why it was essential that he finish it in India (he carted it in a semi-complete state all the way from Brooklyn), but I must confess I failed to follow his logic.

There are many Indians here too, of course. This afternoon the Ramakrishna Mission had a tea party, and I wore my sari. The sweepers outside my door helped me adjust the sari to their approval, then smiled and clucked, and a lovely girl from Madras showed me a very clever way to make double pleats. Somehow the sari is cooler and more fun than non-Indian clothes, and I will wear my two beautiful saris—one mustard yellow with a flame orange blouse, the other shocking pink with pink blouse—whenever it is not the rainy season, or I am travelling.

At the tea the Swami and I spoke Sanskrit together, to our mutual delight, and I was handed round as the scholar from Harvard. Everyone is terribly impressed with my Sanskrit and my burgeoning Bengali!

Nabaneeta has accompanied me on all my shopping excursions—I bought a bedroll and mosquito netting for Shantiniketan—and can't get over having me here.

The Americans tell each other what they do for dysentery.

We took a walk around a lake near here, with perfectly enormous fishes (four feet long, and very fat) bumping each other as thick as the schools of minnows at Shelter Island, and peacocks walking and strange birds crying out, and women bathing themselves and their saris at once (the Indians are at once the most prudish, the most erotic, and the most matter-of-fact people when it comes to nudity, just as they are the most peaceful and the most warlike), and uncircumcised little boys running around, teasing the monkeys, and water buffalo sunk in the mud until you could only see their heads, and a lovely mosque on a lush island in the middle of the lake, with a swinging bridge leading to it, and there, in the midst of all this tropical splendour, I saw groups of men in the reedy water at the edge of the lake, holding up their dhotis and feeling around the bottom with their toes, then suddenly stooping down and coming up with mussels in their hands. I wished I could have talked with them about clamming, but my Bengali isn't that good yet.

I was in a hurry this afternoon, and there were no taxis, and the bearer insisted that I take a rickshaw, and I told him no, but it was too late, and the rickshaw was pulled by a little boy smaller than Tony, and I couldn't stand it, and got out, much to the bearer's amazement. Everyone says that it isn't hard for them and they need the money, but I would never take one again.

Tomorrow I go to Shantiniketan, which is very beautiful, very peaceful, very quiet, very ancient Indian, classes outdoors, music and dancing and weaving and the darling of all Bengalis, and I will write from there soon.

4. *August 17, 1963,*
16, Birla Hostel, Vidya Bhavan, Visva-Bharati,
Shantiniketan, Bolpur, West Bengal

A funny thing happened to me on the way to* the ashram last night. I went into the non-vegetarian restaurant at the famous Howrah station, and the strangest, most Pickwickian Englishman approached me, asked me if I were American, then said, 'Ah, you want fish and chips,' brought them to me, gave me a bottle of catsup that looked ordinary enough but makes nasi goreng seem like rice pudding, spice-wise, and then told me the story of his life. As I finished, I tried to make the bearer understand that I wanted my check, and I couldn't, and I had to make the train for Shantiniketan right away, and in the midst of my frustration I thought of Daddy's International Check Sign,† and made it to him, and he nodded, and a few minutes later seemed to be doing nothing about it, so I raised my eyebrows in inquiry, and goddamned if he didn't reassure me by making the International Check Sign right back at me, and then brought me the check. Perhaps someday someone will get a PhD in psychology for a thesis on the international brotherhood of man as demonstrated by the universality of the sign for 'Check, please'.

In Calcutta, the signs have all decayed, so you have to ask directions, but everyone gives you directions whether or not he knows anything about it, so you mustn't ask. In finding the train for Shantiniketan, for instance, I devised

---

* This is a reference to the musical *A Funny Thing Happened to Me On the Way to the Forum*, that played on Broadway in 1962.

† Holding up one hand and scribbling on it with the other.

a system which, to protect the innocent, I shall call Indian Roulette. I asked the man who sold me the ticket what platform the train would leave from. He said [platform] five. There was no train at five, but there was a train at four. I asked the bearers (carrying my luggage on their heads, probably grateful for the pliant fiberglass) whether the train at four was the Shantiniketan train or not. Two said yes, one said no. Then I asked someone on the train already. He said no. The policeman said yes, a miscellaneous passer-by said yes. A lightning calculation told me that the ayes had a slight majority, so I took the train, and it did go to Shantiniketan. But there must be an easier way.

On the train I met a Bengali man who recited some Tagore poems for me and then told me that he had studied English literature. I hardly had to twist his arm at all, and he came out with, I swear to God, 'The curfew tolls the knell of parting day',* and he got it right, though I think that by this time I have got it wrong again.

All these things have reminded me of my home, and until I got to Shantiniketan, I found myself reminding myself that it was just a few hours' trip home by jet any time I wanted, and that there were just 325 days to go. Now that I have actually begun life here at Shantiniketan, learning many delightful things, proudly adjusting to a new life, making many lovely new friends, I am no longer homesick, but you cannot imagine how very different in many subtle ways the life here is from the life at home. The physical adjustments are very easy for me to make: you will soon

---

* The first line of Thomas Gray's 'Elegy Written in a Country Churchyard'.

hear what a comfortable place this is, and I have always been able to make do with less before. And intellectually, of course, it is the most fascinating and stimulating place I have ever known. But I cannot hear Brahms, or read the *Times,* or go to the movies (Indian movies are something else again, of which more later), and I have discovered that it is only as an American, not as a play Indian, that I can really absorb the many strange things this country has to tell me.

Before I tell you about Shantiniketan, I must tell you all about Calcutta, not just because I went there first, but because it is impossible to understand the psychology of one without the other. Shantiniketan is an ashram, a retreat, but in the full sense of the word, a retreat from Calcutta, and that is why Tagore loved it so much, and that is why I love it, and that is why Indians have always loved retreats, places to escape from Indian life. To a certain extent, for the English, India itself was a retreat from England, from the climate and the pace and the formality, and I am glad that I stopped at London on my way to Calcutta: the English have certainly left their mark, though more on Calcutta than on Shantiniketan, and it is easier now for me to weed it out.

When you walk through the streets of Calcutta, and see the people, diseased and possessing only a white cloth which only approximately covers their genitalia and only sometimes covers the breasts of the women, and there are perhaps five thousand people within your sight, all of them staring at you, all of them Indian, then it is a bit terrifying. And then, too, the situation here is such that in terms of *things* the life is expensive and unsatisfying, but there are thousands of people at hand who, for a coin you would not stoop to pick up in America, would gladly wash your feet and serve your meals and carry you on their backs wherever you want to go. It is a temptation to take advantage of this, to make up in labour for what you are denied in things. And many people even now are unable to resist this temptation: the non-Indians here fall into two categories, the off-beat and the bastards.* Why India has been proclaimed as the home of universal brotherhood, why it is in fact the home of Ramakrishna, is difficult to tell, though the former is more difficult than the latter. But I am grateful to the English for at least one thing: language. Indian English is a tongue unto itself, it is true, but it is far easier to pick up than Bengali or Hindi, and anyway many of the Indians speak neither Bengali nor Hindi, even in Calcutta, and without *some* way of communication the first few days would be impossible.

It seems that the Doniger luck has followed me to India. I have been neither sick nor robbed in all the time I have been in Calcutta and Shantiniketan, and Calcutta, as you may have gathered, is a pretty rough place. An unspoiled first week in India is an achievement far more impressive than climbing Everest or even getting into Radcliffe. It is universally agreed that I am now over the danger point, so you can all relax. Moreover, there have been no snakes (venomous) or malaria at Shantiniketan for twenty-five years. So there. I have been careful, though not paranoid,

---

* Translating my younger self now, I think I meant that the American tourists were either hippies (remember, this was the '60s) or capitalist types that exploited cheap labour.

about food, which means more or less living on vitamin pills and hard-boiled eggs and Coca-Cola in Calcutta, but at Shantiniketan the water is pure, which is quite a blessing (I'll never forget the moment when I froze, hand on toothbrush in mouth, and realized that I had just brushed my teeth in Calcutta tap water, the kind they wash the corpses in. But nothing happened, except a temporary loss of appetite, purely psychological; now that I am at ease here, I think it is all a myth, a matter of attitude, but then, I am no longer in Calcutta), as it is really quite difficult to boil all the water you use for *everything*, including washing dishes. But psychological or not, the fear of pollution plagues all visitors to Calcutta, and the sight of a First Class Waiting Room is really a great relief: you want to have a place to be clean, and uncrowded, and unstared at for a moment.

Getting to Shantiniketan was a tale in itself. I had to go to the bank: at first they said they had never heard of me. Man geht zum Schmidt,* so I asked to see the president, who came from Iowa, and he went right in and brought me my money in half an hour, a task which is a standard four hour job in Calcutta: you have to bring a book to read when you cash a check. But I think I have gotten to the bottom of the psychology of Indian bureaucracy: it's just curiosity. At the airport, for instance, I wasn't asked to open any of my suitcases, but I had my travelling case open for my documents, and I had a Tampax in it, and I could not leave the customs table until I had explained the theory and

* One of my mother's Viennese sayings: '*Man geht nicht zum Schmidl, man geht zum Schmidt*', or, 'You don't go to the little smith, you go to the Smith,' i.e. the big man, the man in charge. See *The Donigers of Great Neck.*

practice of Tampax to all the Air India stewardesses. They just had to know. As I began this letter, a little girl walked into my room and examined the typewriter, the drawers of my desk, and everything else that caught her fancy. She then said, 'Good morning' (it is 7 pm), salaamed, and left. So with bureaucracy: every single person in the establishment must read the entire document in question, commenting upon it minutely: 'Ah, Sanskrit! You are a pandit! I know a little Sanskrit: "*Dharmakshetre kurukshetre*" [The beginning of the *Bhagavad Gita*] ... Ah, Shantiniketan! A beautiful place. I have never been there. So, New York! I have a brother in Yugoslavia. You are only twenty-two? So young to be travelling alone! You must visit the Punjab. That is my home. I hope you will enjoy your stay in India...[etc.] Namaskar.' This conversation must take place with each of the twenty-five clerks who have to sign the document, and I am convinced that the only reason that all twenty-five have to sign it is that they all want to read it and talk to you. The whole process took me twice as long at first because, after we got everything all straight, and I would ask him if I could go, he would shake his head, and I would go through the whole list, and he would shake his head for each item, where before he had said it was alright. After some pretty amazing charades I discovered that a Bengali shakes his head to say Yes. I then took to forging all the signatures myself, as nobody reads them, and you have no idea how it expedites matters. Ed Dimock, who is practically a native, refused to believe that I had cashed a check in less than an hour. But I have found that the people here are overflowing with kindness, though frequently unable to understand what you want (or, in such matters as toilet paper or pure water, to believe that you really want it), and a little bit of patience and ingenuity in communication is worth a great deal.

Forgive the long digression in the tale of my trip to Shantiniketan, but you might look upon it as a subtle literary device to express the pace and character of the trip itself, indeed of all aspects of Indian life.

Even the Bengalis consider the Shantiniketan food [in the dormitory] execrable. It consists *entirely* of rice, bread, potatoes, one egg per day, tea, biscuits, and a sharp sauce. Well, after one day I went to see the cook at the guest house, and, with the help of my friend and interpreter [Chanchal] (about whom more later) arranged to have lunch and dinner sent over (the guest house is a mile away) in a tiffin carrier, each day, to my room. Lunch now consists of a good soup, braised liver, mixed vegetables, fish cakes, cucumber salad, bread, bananas, and parsley potatoes. Dinner is soup, chicken (roast or broiled or curried or fried) or mutton, vegetables, fruit, pudding, and cookies. And for all this I pay the staggering sum of $25 a month. Of course, twenty-five people had to sign my petition for meals at the guest house, but by now I have come to think of it as a rather pleasant way to spend a morning in friendly conversation, getting a document 'finalized' as the Bengalis call it (though I suppose it's 'finalised').

The Viennese[*] are speed demons compared to the

---

[*] My mother was Viennese, and they are notoriously late for everything and slowpokes (especially compared with the Germans). See *The Donigers of Great Neck.*

Bengalis. And I must confess that I like it very much. It takes all the nervousness out of life, and lets you sit back and enjoy everything. And there is a great deal to enjoy here; if the people create for themselves what would seem to an American an inordinate amount of leisure, they do fill that leisure with things that most Americans have not yet come to value—embroidery, and the study of scriptures, arranging flowers, carving, telling stories, playing with children (the parents, both of them, seem to do nothing else) and fressing.* The Bengalis are always nibbling on something—a betel nut, or a leaf filled with *pan*, or a sweetmeat, or a sort of cottage cheese candy; everywhere on the streets you see children wearing nothing but a string under the stomach, following you curiously with their eyes while their heads are held motionless by their mothers who are popping little things to eat into their mouths.

Forgive the wild non-construction of that last sentence, but I am the only one here who speaks English as a native language, and it is beginning to take its toll already. The Bengalis say, 'Is it?' when they mean 'Really!' or, I guess, 'N'est-ce pas?', though I really don't know what the French ever had to do with Bengal, except to produce the best books about its erotic sculpture, naturellement. The movies are referred to as flims [*sic*] and amidst all the bedlam of various patois (people are here from all over Asia) it is quite startling to come upon such common phrases as 'class-wise', 'Train Tickets Cum Reservations', and 'You

---

* A Yiddish word, derived from the German verb *fressen*, which means to eat like an animal. In Yiddish, it means to eat constantly and indiscriminately, promiscuously.

may go now' in the more obscure and archaic sense in which it is used here, namely, to signify 'Please have a seat'. So I'm afraid that every yard I gain in Bengali is a two-yard loss in English. And the Bengali book I have is all wrong: nowhere does it tell you how to say, 'The lunch you cooked for me was delicious', 'Thank you for going to such trouble for me', 'You needn't have done that for me', and 'Thank you for showing me how to do that'. Even in Calcutta, when I stayed at the Ramakrishna Mission, the Swami gave me a copy of his book, inscribed with love, and the sweeper sang a song for me in the most beautiful voice, and no one has allowed me to carry anything heavier than a pencil since I arrived.

(*Continued in Part III*)

Part Three

SHANTINIKETAN

My classes at Shantiniketan seldom took place at all. Shantiniketan prided itself on the fact that the classes were held under the trees. But as it was monsoon season when I was there, there was often a torrential outburst when we were to meet under the trees for the class, and so we raced back into the building to find an empty classroom. Since everyone else was doing the same thing, by the time we found a classroom the hour for the class was over. This happened day after day. Finally, I suggested that we might actually just *meet* in a classroom, but I was told, 'In Shantiniketan, the classes are held under the trees.' So we went back to (not) meeting under the trees.

I did manage, however, to study both Bengali and Sanskrit, not in classes but in private lessons. The Sanskrit texts that I worked on there—and that remained the basic library on which I drew for my research for many years—were the Puranas, medieval Sanskrit compendia of mythology that historians had mined for items of (generally non-factual) history but that scholars of mythology had largely neglected. I loved the Puranas and used them as my main texts of mythology right from the start. Later, when I came to live in Calcutta, I studied the Puranas with Rajendra Chandra Hazra, who was more a historian than a mythologist but knew all about the Puranas, on which he had published several foundational books. Born in

1905, he would have been just fifty-eight in 1963, but he seemed old to me in my callow twenty-third year. In Shantiniketan I apparently worked with a scholar named Lahe, said to be Hazra's star pupil, but I have been unable to find out anything more about him, not even his first name. Moreover, though I say in one letter (September 3, 1963) that he had arrived at Shantiniketan, a later letter (September 15, 1963) says he was *supposed* to arrive at that time but was delayed and only arrived later, and in the interim I worked with another, unnamed pandit. This sort of confusion was endemic in the circles in which I moved in India, often in circles.

At Shantiniketan we used to recite, every morning, a poem from the *Shvetashvatara Upanishad* that I refer to (September 3, 1963) as an 'old Vedic poem about the spirit that dwells in the leaves and in the waters, and about the sanctity of all life'. It goes:

Yo dev' agnau, yo'psu,
yo vishvam bhuvanam avivesha.
Yo' aushadishu. Yo vanaspatishu.
Tasmai devaya namo namah.
Om, shanti shanti shanti. Hari om.

Translated:

The god who is in fire, who is in the waters,
who has entered into the entire universe,
who is in the grasses and in the trees
—we bow, we bow to that god.
Peace, peace, peace, O Lord.

I also studied the *mangals*, long, often epic poems in Bengali, that wove together folktales and myths of the gods. And I learned two Tagore songs that I still remember, and from time to time have sung with my Bengali colleague Dipesh Chakravarti: 'Jokhon Eshechile' and 'Akash Bhora Surjo Tara'. I can also still have conversations with Bengali taxi drivers. But, alas, I no longer read Bengali literature.

I very much regret that I no longer have my notes on my Sanskrit studies nor more than a few of the hundreds of photographs I took in India. In one letter (September 3, 1963) I remark that 'I'll keep my notes with me, as I refer to them constantly'. And since I did not send them to my mother, who would have kept them with the letters, I do not have those notes now. I am also very, very sorry that I can find no trace of any of the photographs from my year in India except for one of myself and my mother in Mahabalipuram (which we've used for the cover of this book), one of myself in Kathmandu with a nun (see page 251) to whom Penelope Betjeman had introduced me, one of my mother holding a large python in Benares (see page 250), one of my friend Mishtuni Roy at the Taj Mahal (see page 167), one of my friend Chanchal with the Prime Minister of India (see page 201), one of a Kathakali troop performing in a village in the hills above Madras (see page 249), and one of my mother at Konark (see page 248). I took rolls and rolls of photographs throughout my time in India, but somehow I lost all but these. I also have a photograph of myself in late March of that year, when I had returned home and was married in a white, gold-encrusted Benarsi sari (see page 15).

There are references in the letters to ballet and to choral singing. In my teens, I had studied ballet with George Balanchine and modern dance with Martha Graham and Anna Sokolow. At ballet school in America, we identified our teachers by saying, 'I take from Balanchine,' a phrase I then applied in India (August

30, 1963) to the teacher with whom I studied Manipuri dancing at Shantiniketan, whom we called 'Mastaji' (Honoured Master). Manipur is a province in Northeast India that has a distinct form of dancing, gentler and easier than Bharatanatyam. As part of my travels in India (a part that did not get into the letters), I also met Balasaraswati, the great South Indian dancer and teacher of Bharatanatyam, and was allowed to attend several of her master classes, though I never properly studied with her.

As for choral singing, when I was at Radcliffe, I sang with the Handel and Haydn Society in Boston, and I had sung in the chorus when Benjamin Britten's *War Requiem* was performed for the first time in America, by the Boston Symphony Orchestra at Tanglewood, with Erich Leinsdorf conducting, on July 27, 1963, shortly before I flew to India. I refer to this experience in one of the letters (September 3, 1963) because it explains how I could understand some of the irregularities of Indian music.

In that same letter, I refer to a bird singing a most unusual song. On another occasion, when I was walking outside with a Bengali friend, I heard that bird singing and called my friend's attention to it and asked her the name of the bird. 'Oh,' said she, 'that's a *pakkhi*.' Thrilled that I had at last identified this mysterious songbird, I returned to my dorm to try to ascertain the English equivalent of *pakkhi*. 'Oh,' said the first person I asked, '*pakkhi* means "bird",' as I should have known, since *pakshi* is the Sanskrit for 'bird'. So I never found out the English name of that bird.

∼

4. August 17, 1963 (Continued)

But now I really must tell you about Shantiniketan. Having managed to get myself and all my luggage on the right train (a tale full of sound and fury), I arrived at Bolpur (the sign on the station spelled it Bolepur, the post office spells it Bolpure, the people at the University spell it Bolpur—life is very approximate here) after having had tea served on the train. There being no corridors but rather compartments, English style, the man serving the tea had to actually scramble along the [out]side of the moving train, holding on to windows and handles, all the while balancing a tray in one hand, like a scene from a Harold Lloyd movie,[*] and dashing into the compartment just in time to avoid being squashed against a tunnel we were entering, while the engineer blew the whistle loudly, as he did in every tunnel, like the children at the zoo.

Arriving at Bolpur in the evening, I was met by a delegation from Shantiniketan (everyone had warned me that when I arrived at Shantiniketan no one would have heard of me, and I would probably have to sleep in the street: this was diametrically opposed to the true case, as you will see. I heard all sorts of untrue rumours about Shantiniketan while I was in Calcutta. It is a place of great controversy, because the Bengalis are great hero-worshippers, and Shantiniketan is a shrine to Tagore, and the Bengalis are also great iconoclasts, so opinion differs widely. You will soon see which class I fall into) consisting of a girl from Trinidad and a girl from Thailand. They put

---

[*] Harold Lloyd (1913–1963) was a silent-movie actor famous for insanely dangerous daredevil stunts.

me and my bags into a kind of rickshaw pulled by a boy on a bicycle, the only means of transportation out here besides bullock, and told me that everyone had been waiting for me to come for two weeks already, and that my room was all ready and everyone dying to meet me. And it has been that way ever since. As I began to type this page, Yubon, the Thai girl (pronounced 'tiger', much to my confusion at first) who lives next door, brought me a bowl of lotuses and asked me how to pronounce 'luxurious'; Chat Su, who is also Thai, gave me a special Thai sauce to put on my rice. The night I arrived, I was unpacked, mosquito netted (you drape a sort of canopy over the bed, giving a lovely, airy, safe feeling, like being in a crib, or sleeping in the summer palace of a king; I have always loved to crawl under things and go to sleep), briefed, questioned, admired, all in a great flurry of girlish curiosity.

I live in the Scholars' Block, Birla Hostel (room 16, for the mail boy), where most of the foreign (that is, non-Bengali) girls live, Chinese, Punjabi, Trinidadian, Persian, South Indian, and Japanese. I am the only American here. Being foreigners, we have many special concessions: we live in the newest hostel (five months old), have showers and toilets and good, soft American-style toilet paper, don't have to play games (which is a damn good thing, as they are held at 5 every morning: as it is I get up at 6, but am already accustomed to it). Classes are from 7 to 11 and from 2 to 6, to avoid the hot part of the day. I have only two classes, Bengali and music (that is singing and dancing), but I rise with the others to go to morning prayers, when we stand in the forest and sing the ancient and, I have discovered, beautiful hymn, 'Om, Shanti, Shanti, Shanti'. I am also learning Tagore songs. But I digress.

I made an immediate friend of a girl from South India, who is studying painting here and to do so has had to be away from her husband, who lives in Delhi, where she visits him over vacation. She loves him very much, and misses him, and I told her all about how I met my fiancé, and she told me all about how she met her husband, and I suddenly realized that she had met him at her wedding, of course, and yet our feelings were so very much the same. She was married a year ago and came here only two months later; the girls call her Bhabhi, sister-in-law, and tease her, and she blushes furiously. I am not yet teased, but I am told that my boyfriend looks very big and strong, a remark which is followed by wild shrieks of laughter and a babble of multilingual comments. It is, of course, a girls' dormitory, an institution from which I have been known to go to the most extreme measures to escape, but it is more than saved for me because the girls are all extremely innocent and bright and happy and generous and friendly and, though they seem much younger than Americans of the same age, dignified, and dignity is the one quality which makes it possible to live close to people. Some of them do speak English quite well, and when they do it is none of the malicious, small, spoiled, and usually quite obscene gossiping that so characterized my alma mater, but talk of their countries, and their studies, and what they hope for in life, and things that strike them as funny, and all the things I like to talk about. I was also quite pleasantly surprised to find that they are all crazy about America and

56

AN AMERICAN GIRL IN INDIA

Americans: I expected to be a dirty word in India, but not so. A lot of it is, of course, material: 'Some Thai things are good,' Yubon agreed when I admired her dress, 'but all American things are good.' But it's more than that. It would seem that Americans have been more friendly and interested and generous and accommodating than the other non-Indians they have met; perhaps I will be able to find out more about it, but for the time being I'm not going to look a gift horse in the mouth.

Things here are very simple and beautiful. I have put away all my good dresses and wear only one or two rayon ones. When the rains stop, I will wear saris and Punjabi dress (pants and a long tunic with a chiffon drape at the shoulder). Dinner is served in a cool hall with long wooden benches and metal plates and cups. My room has a bed with a bright orange spread and white netting canopy, a large cabinet for my clothes and toilet articles, which is metal and locks, a desk with a brass vase filled with peacock feathers, books in a pair of sandalwood bookends, a sandalwood frame for photographs, a bowl of lotuses, replenished with a different colour lotus cluster every day, a chair, and that's about it. At night, the bearer comes in with a stove of incense that drives out the insects while I am out, and then I burn punk, good old punk, which takes care of them while I am asleep. There are a great many insects of unbelievable dimensions, and the lizards grow long and fat on them. Only now can I fully appreciate the sacrifice made by the Jains in wearing gauze masks to keep from destroying any insects: loving these insects really takes a lot of doing.

In the evening, the girls in the Sangeet Bhavan ['Song Block'] ([there was a sign that read:] 'Except in the Sangeet Bhavan, music and dancing is forbidden during study hours') sing and play the sitar. Everywhere girls are painting in the classical style, some copying famous miniatures, some sketching the cranes down at the lake. There are beautiful, strange trees and flowers outside my window, and exquisite birds and funny little cat-like goats, and skinny cows with soft eyes, not like our cows at all, and at night the jackals howl for about an hour, an indescribable sound like a cross between the yowl of a tomcat and the baying of a hound and the mooing of a frightened cow. And, much to my pleasant surprise, the afternoons are filled with the sounds of children. Shantiniketan is really a little colony and teaches kindergarten as well as graduate school; there is no school in the afternoon, and so there is a lot of scurrying and singing and crying and screaming and chanting and falling down, and all the sounds that I most like to hear outside my window when I am pretending to work. At night, there are so many stars that it would be easier to count the patches of blue than to count them. The Milky Way is like a great white chiffon scarf, or, as the Indians used to believe, like the Ganges flowing through heaven on its way to earth. I counted a hundred shooting stars from my window last night, in just a few minutes. It is quite cool at night, with breezes, and everyone makes tea for everyone else.

As for my official reception here, they did everything short of a ticker-tape parade. Harvard is a glorious name to them. A Sanskrit scholar is almost as rare here as in

America, though much more honoured. The president* uncrossed his legs, straightened his Gandhi cap, and bowed low to me, then introduced me to the faculty, including some Tagore descendants. When they received my application they had no one on the staff who was a specialist in Puranic literature, though they had several who would have been able to help me, so they wrote to Professor Hazra (the world expert on Puranas; I met him in Calcutta before I came out here, unexpectedly, because when I went to Mukhopadhyaya, the most famous Calcutta bookseller, and he discovered that I was interested in Puranas, he immediately telephoned Hazra and had his servant bring me to Hazra's house. Hazra was very helpful, told me where to start and what to consider, etc., and very smiley) and got Hazra's star pupil (Hazra is a very old man) and engaged him to come to teach at Shantiniketan for this year. And if that isn't a real reception, what is? In January, Nehru is coming here (he is the chancellor of Shantiniketan) and I will meet him.

So you see what a lovely place this is. Chat Su and I were telling each other how much we loved it, and she said, 'You don't need very much. Calm is the most useful thing.' Useful is not a word I would have thought of, but it is the right word. The calm here would be unnatural, ivory-towerish anywhere but in India, where it is as much a form of real life as the jungles and cities from which it is a retreat. Here everything good is preserved, everything bad discarded or set right. The girls are all very beautiful

---

* I have absolutely no idea what he was president of.

and must think me either a shutterbug or a lesbian (if they have such a concept at all) for continually photographing them. (I will finish the roll and send it home, undeveloped, tomorrow.) Even the animals are strangely tame here; perhaps the smell of vegetarian cooking sets them at ease. In October there is a month's vacation, and six of us will take a trip to Delhi, where Pushparatri lives,* and visit Agra and Khajuraho and Jaipur from there. They have all been to Agra, but they want me to see it with them.

This will probably be the last letter of such generous proportions. I wanted to tell you all about Shantiniketan, and as my classes don't begin until tomorrow, I had time to write a long one.

5. *August 23, 1963,*
Shantiniketan

Now I am very busy, learning Sanskrit and Bengali and Manipuri dancing and meeting all sorts of people and walking around the countryside and generally living it up, and I only have time for a short letter. Mostly news.

I have sent the first rolls of film, all taken at Shantiniketan. If many of them seem to be of me, it's because everyone insisted that I be immortalized in sari in formal pose à la Indian miniatures. In one or two, if you look closely, you will see the classes held under the trees. Others are pictures of my friends (if they look glum, it's because they consider being photographed a most formal occasion, and refuse to smile). One of the first will be of

* Pushparatri does not reappear in my letters and I do not remember who she was.

a building with wrought iron windows and gate; that is where I live.

I have been in perfect health all along. At dinnertime the mosquitoes come out, and I feel a bit like the middle fish, being eaten while eating (the more so as I occasionally find myself eating a bug or two), but perhaps my flesh is not spicy enough for their taste, for I find that they pretty much leave me alone. Since I get up at 5:30, and my first meal is brought at 11, I pass the morning on my good old academic staple, peanut butter sandwiches and tea.

I was invited to have tea with the Tagores, who live here (descendants of Rabindranath); he teaches Chinese and she, a perfectly delightful woman, educated at Oxford, has written a book of Bengali folk tales. She has sent them to one publisher of children's books in America, who found them too bloody for American children. I suggested that she publish them for adults, India-philes, anthropologists, folk-niks and the like. She was very pleased with this idea, and I wonder if you would be interested in them? Somewhere at home or Shelter Island is Ed Dimock's book of Bengali tales, *The Thief of Love*, in a purple jacket. Hers are something like the shorter tales in that volume, but mostly about animals. Tell me what you think.

The Tagores have given me the names of several auction houses in Calcutta where you get the best Indian miniatures at the best price. I trust that all my training at Parke-Bernet will hold me in good stead. There is altogether too much going on here to tell you in a letter. I am deeply impressed with the fascinating charm of the place. Someday I will tell you all about it, but for now suffice it to say that I am well, learning many, many things, scholastic and human, completely adapted to all the little ways of the place, pampered, amused, having a wonderful time, your obedient servant, Wendy Doniger, Esq.

6. *August 28, 1963,*
Shantiniketan

This is not a worldly place; that is why I like it so much. The first I heard of Nehru being booed or Madame Pandit replacing Krishna Menon or any of that was from reading your letter, so I beg you to keep me informed on Indian politics. As for the Chinese, I know about that and there is nothing to be worried about, honest. Not even the Indians fear an invasion; if there ever should be one, geography prohibits its taking place before January, and if they should do anything then, I would have plenty of time to get to Delhi from here without going through Calcutta. So fear not. I am not foolhardy, and will hop home at the first hint of danger.

I have made a wonderful new friend. Her name is Mishtuni [Roy], and she is a very beautiful Bengali girl (though she doesn't think so, because she is very dark, and the Bengalis, through a combination of British and Brahmin influences, only consider light complexions beautiful). We took a long bus ride to a neighbouring village, riding through the flooded paddy fields and lotus ponds and herds of goats and cows, and even saw two dancing bears, and on the way I discovered that she sings folk songs very beautifully, and knows many lovely Indian songs and Tagore poems and Sanskrit poems and wonderful stories about Shiva, and loves Shiva just the way I do. And she knows and loves and understands and quotes profusely Robert Frost and e. e. cummings and Winnie the Pooh and James Joyce and *Alice in Wonderland* and Yeats, all my favourites, and is even an avid James Baldwin fan (could you send *Another Country* by book post?). I was so starved for English poetry, and she is teaching me some beautiful poems by D.H. Lawrence and Emily Dickinson that I didn't know. She loves all the right things about America, the poets and the New England seasons and the Grand Canyon, and loves them even though she has a sharp understanding of the terrible lapse of values, so that I was really proud of America with her, and taught her (among many other songs which she loved) 'America the Beautiful' and the 'Battle Hymn of the Republic'. She has asked me to sing and explain some American songs at a big song festival that she has organized. What a wonderful ride we had, singing and reciting the poems we both knew, she in a lovely Indian accent, and swapping stories about Shiva.

In October is the festival of Durga Puja, which celebrates the time when Uma, the wife of Shiva, comes home to visit her mother for the first time after her wedding to Shiva. Her mother weeps to see her, calling her her little girl, getting her sari all tangled up in her confusion, and saying, 'Oh, he is not good enough for my darling. Why, he didn't even come home with you. Why did I ever let you marry him? I know he is a god, but he is a beggar. I know he is handsome, but he is so unconventional. I know he is well dressed, but he wears so little. I'll bet he doesn't even make enough money to feed you properly.' Uma smiles and says nothing, but after four days Shiva comes to take her back again, saying that he cannot live without her even for another day.* And so she goes with him, and that is the end of the main part of the festival. So you see, it is the same all over. That is the way that parents are about daughters, even if they marry gods.

I am well, well fed, well befriended, and learning a great deal of fascinating things. Now I must have my dinner.

7. *August 30, 1963,*
Shantiniketan

I have begun my dance classes here. It's a lovely kind of dancing, and, although my hands don't bend backwards, I find that grace and balance and control are the pillars of Manipuri dance as they were of ballet and modern. I am proving, much to the surprise of the dance master (but not of my doting parents, I am sure), very good at it.

The big studio, the strict dance master, who even carries a little bamboo stick with which he emphasizes your mistakes, the pleasant feeling of being hot and wet clear through, the 1, 2, 3, 4—all of it conspires to make me feel like the old days again, and I almost want to say that 'I take from Mastaji'. I wear Punjabi costume, a shocking pink tunic and harem pants (made for me by a tailor for a dollar), and I will buy a real Manipuri costume when I am in Delhi. I am so glad to be dancing again, I will keep it up (if not in Manipuri, then at least in modern) when I go back home. And there is a special system of dance notation that I am learning, so as not to forget it.

---

* I wrote about this tradition at some length in *Siva: The Erotic Ascetic* (1973).

Random notes: a girl who in America would be said to have 'no chic' is here said to 'wear her sari as a horse would wear it'.

Everything here is wrapped in newsprint, which disintegrates within an hour. I use plastic bags for everything—sometimes I even drink out of them. Only if you knew how many of the things we take for granted are unheard of here could you know what saviours the plastic bags are.

Yesterday I saw a group of little Bengali girls playing hopscotch (potsy, if you will) in exactly the kind of potsy court that you painted for me [at home when I was little].

Tonight is the Varshamangal, the festival of the rains, welcoming them. In true Indian fashion it is being celebrated tonight, now that the monsoon is almost over (it began in June), but it is supposed to be very beautiful.

Last night we were all sitting around singing and they asked me to teach them some American songs, and after a few they asked me to teach them 'You Can Kiss Me On A Monday', and I said I was sorry but I didn't know it and they said they had loved the movie, and I realized suddenly that they meant 'Never on Sunday'. Whoever said that the Indians weren't positive thinkers?

I knew that I would be considered the representative of whatever religion I chose to espouse, and after being showered with pictures of lurid Jesuses and Pulpit-Digesty prayer reprints, I finally broke down and declared myself one of the chosen people, much to everyone's delight, for they have *never* seen a Jew (though someone's cousin knows one) and are amazed that my hair is blond and my nose small. So I have been setting everyone straight, and teaching them Shalom Chaverim [a Jewish song that Pete Seeger used to sing] ('Shalom is Shanti,' they realized), and telling them that, contrary to general Shantiniketan belief, Nasser is *not* the president of Israel, and all Jews do *not* live in Israel, and all in all it has been pretty hilarious and I enjoy it as much as they do, which is a great deal.

At night, the boys in Kala Bhavan ('Fine Arts Block') have gotten together a most peculiar little orchestra, consisting of a sitar, a tabla (drum), a guitar and a harmonica, and they sing parodies of the Tagore songs, which, in this temple to Tagore, is about equivalent, sacrilege-wise, to jazzing up Hail Marys in a monastery.

Yubon, the little Thai girl next door, has shown me how to drape a sarong and how to say Goodbye and Please and Love in Thai dance figures, and how to make a swan or a monkey or a rose out of a handkerchief, in return for which I teach her English. Most of the people here are majoring in English literature, but none of the professors speak English even brokenly, and the students, who can barely say 'How are you?', are immediately set to work reading Ruskin essays and 'Samson Agonistes'. But they all love it, and I correct their homework without cracking a smile. The little boys follow me around saying 'Good Morning' all day, and asking me for stamps, which I give them.

8. September 3, 1963,
Shantiniketan

The Bengalis have a saying called 'The Maxim of the Barber's Son', which is a reference to a story about a king who asked his barber to bring him the most beautiful boy in the country. The barber searched and searched, and finally came home weary and discouraged, and saw his own son playing in the yard. Rejoicing, he took him to the king and said, 'This is the most beautiful boy in the kingdom.' He was hunchbacked and scrawny and homely, but the king rewarded the barber for his wise choice. It's just like the Russian story, 'My Mother is the Most Beautiful Woman in the World',* isn't it?

At dinner the other night the cook served some delicious eggplant, and I asked him if I could have it more often. 'Egg plant?' he said, not understanding. Then, after a meditative pause, he broke into a smile of comprehension and said, 'Oh! You mean *chicken!*'

You know, I could hardly be called an avid newspaper reader, but now I have found several newspapers written in Bengali, and I have been reading them to practise my Bengali, and I have suddenly contracted a terrible longing to read the *New York Times* and find out what is going on in India. (Bengali newspapers just tell about Bengal, unless someone swipes the international section before I get to it, which is possible, and even the national news is stuck in an obscure corner, to make way for Swami Vivekananda's meditation upon the Upanishads, and reports of Bengali prowess in musical competitions.)

My Sanskrit professor, Lahe, has finally arrived, and he is a Great Man. The department head here (who has been directing my research in Lahe's absence, and directing it

* A book, published by Russian War Relief, that my mother had given me.

very well, too) does obeisance, and Lahe knows exactly how to go about inspiring and teaching. Up to now I have been doing a great deal of everything but Sanskrit, but now I am working on the Puranas, and they really are the most fun of all. You will have to wait and read about them in my book, I'm afraid; I'll keep my notes with me, as I refer to them constantly.

This is just going to be a jumble of notes, because I haven't got time (as the lady* says) to write a short letter. But perhaps it will have a sort of whirlwind effect, which is the right effect.

I am really learning Bengali. I can read some Tagore songs and poems, and am learning the tunes, too: most of them are in a seven-beat rhythm, for which I have been prepared by the Britten *Requiem*, which has a lot of seven-fourth measures, and as I hear the Bengalis singing them as easily if they were waltzes I remember Erich Leinsdorf admonishing us to count, '1, 2, 3, 1, 2, 3, 4' as it was impossible to *feel* 7, even for him. Difficult for him, but easy for Indians.†

I am experiencing all sorts of strange linguistic problems: the woman who does my washing kept wringing

---

* The quote which I here attributed, tongue in cheek, to an unnamed lady is from Blaise Pascal, who famously remarked (in Letter 16, December 4, 1656, of his *Provincial Letters*), 'I would have written a shorter letter, but I did not have the time.'

† This is a paraphrase from a popular television show in which a Spanish ventriloquist named Señor Wences made his closed hand look like a little person named Johnny and had conversations with him. He also had a box with someone named Pedro in it, to whom he would say, 'Is difficole,' to which Pedro replied, 'Difficole for you, but for me eet is easy.' Or the reverse.

out the drip-dry dresses, so that they dried all crinkled, and I had quite a time explaining the principles of drip-dry to her (I kept thinking of the *Thurber Carnival* lady who wanted to know how to say, 'I flushed my passport,' in French). For some strange reason, my terrific, frustrated desire to communicate in a foreign language occasionally drives me to *any* old foreign language, and I hear myself saying things like, and I quote, '*C'est tomaar?*' (*tomaar* means 'yours' in Bengali) or '*aami baadi gehe*' (*aami* means 'I' and *baadi* means 'home' [and *gehe* is German for 'I am going']). But sometimes I think that they understand my French and German about as well as they understand my Bengali, so what the hell.

There has been a whistling outside my window for the last several nights, exactly like this, very high:

[In the letter here I sketched a five-line staff of music notation, each note repeated twice going up and the last three just once going down:

C, D, E-flat, F, G, F, E, D]

At first I thought it was one of my friends (they sing and whistle and make all sorts of animal noises to call you), but then I discovered that it is actually a little bird, who sings a perfect minor scale up and major scale down, for five notes in perfectly syncopated rhythm. The Indian Ragas, by the way, have both of these scales, and I guess there really is a natural mathematical consistency in the sounds of nature as well as the harmonics of sound frequencies. It still gives me a very eerie feeling, though.

Current Indian joke: 'What is the best religion?' 'Since, by democratic rule, the best is the one with the greatest following, then atheism (Russia and China) is the best.' This is a very bitter joke to an Indian.

You know the Satyajit Ray–Tagore film 'Two Daughters'? Well, here it is 'Three Daughters'. The heroine of one of the stories was killed by religious fanatics, and the Indian censors [for international export, presumably] felt it gave a bad picture of Indian life, I guess (not that the other two picture it as a bed of roses).

I had a long talk with a woman who is studying medicine in Calcutta. She was very enthusiastic about anatomy, particularly about dissection. 'I have my own body to cut up,' she said with sincere enthusiasm. 'You know, bodies are very cheap in India.' Well, if that isn't looking at the positive side of things, I don't know what is.

Last night was full moon, and everyone wore white and walked across the meadows singing a lovely Tagore song about the moon. I have never seen such moonlight. You could easily read by it, and it was difficult to look right at the moon for any length of time. The monsoon clouds swept by it very swiftly, looking starched and solid in the bright, cool light, and the moon was so bright that it cut right through the clouds, so that it looked as if they kept parting before it. And there was a beautiful halo around it even when there were no clouds, and thousands of stars, the dimmest of them brighter than Venus is at home.

It's funny; in spite of all the really foreign and fascinating things here, I am still most interested in and moved by the things I love best at home—the sky, and the children, and the trees. Some of this, paradoxically, is due to the feeling of Shantiniketan itself, which is so tied up in nature—the temple services are held outdoors, and you can see the squirrels and monkeys fighting and the crows stealing things, and the birds shaking drops of water off the flowering trees while you hear the old Vedic poem about the spirit that dwells in the leaves and in the waters, and about the sanctity of all life.

I have been reading a wonderful book by Tagore: *Sadhana* (in English, and highly recommended). He talks about the Indian heritage as one which grew up in forests, while the West has been built in cities ('Man is a creature that lives in cities by his very nature,' said Aristotle, and the Indians feel that everything of a city is unnatural), and that living in cities, in walls, makes you think in terms of walls, in terms of possessing things and guarding them and storing them and keeping people out, while living in forests, without boundaries, makes you *realize* instead of possess. I think there is a great deal to this, and I think this is one of the reasons that I have been shunning cities more and more these last few years, why I could no longer bear to live in New York, and one of the reasons why I love Shantiniketan so much. Of course, I am not wholly a forest dweller; I have my own way of possessing, and that is to possess in memory. I have brought that acquisitiveness with me even here, as witness this very letter, which, aside from an attempt to communicate what is impossible to communicate, is in addition an attempt to preserve what is impossible to preserve: an experience, a moment. That form of acquisitiveness, which is also what makes me want to write a book (Steinbeck says that the same spirit that makes little boys write dirty words in bathrooms makes poets write their books: an urge to prove that we really existed), will follow me to the grave, I'm sure, and I really don't think that the Indians are subject to it in the same way we are in America (though their stone temples still stand, none of the kings had their histories written, none of the poets recorded their songs, with but a few exceptions*) and I know it is foreign to the Indian philosophy, where no individual *does* in fact exist. This is quite afield from trees (you should excuse the metaphor), but you do see the connection, don't you? And it is part of the same feeling that man is just a part of nature, something we *say* we believe, but we don't really. When I first came here, and had to boil all my water, and go to crazy lengths to guard against the insects, and shower twice a day (when there was water) to keep from drowning in my own sweat, I was surprised to hear one of the Bengali girls say, when we were all praising Shantiniketan, 'It is so easy to stay alive here.' For me it was quite a struggle (difficult for me, but for them...). But now I understand what she meant. The insects do eat you, and the water makes you sick, and you get used to being wet all the time, pretending, as I do, that the salty taste of the water is sea water, and that I am still in a wet bathing suit, and when it rains you get wet—and you just do, that's all, and you don't begrudge the insects their food, or even the little amoebas snuggling down in your intestines, and life *is* easier here than anywhere else. Life here is governed by the weather as it is in a fishing village—your whole mood and the boundaries of your

---

* These statements are simply not true, but I believed them then.

activities are controlled by the sun and the rain; you are no worse off than a bird (in America one would say no better off than a bird). Tagore says, 'When man leaves his resting-place in universal nature, when he walks on the single rope of humanity, it means either a dance or a fall for him, he has ceaselessly to strain at every nerve and muscle to keep his balance at each step, and then, in the intervals of his weariness, he fulminates against Providence and feels a secret pride and satisfaction in thinking that he has been unfairly dealt with by the whole scheme of things.'

I find that a sari is after all the best thing to wear, and it has many wonderful uses: you tie up your money in the end of it, use it as a potholder, a towel, a handkerchief, a kerchief, a rain hat, a shawl, a veil, a bag to carry fruit, and just about whatever else you need. I wear my hair in a long braid.

I met an American travelling with the Peace Corps and he told me of a terrible faux pas. It is a great insult to question the purity of the water at your host's house here: the Indians pride themselves upon the purity of their wells as the British upon their lawns, but with less reason, I'm afraid. Most Americans have pills they slip into the water to purify it. Well, at a big and fancy dinner party, this man waited until no one was looking and secretly dropped a pill into his water [...] and the water immediately turned bright orange [it was apparently a chlorine pill, which will do that], much to his chagrin.

There is a girl here who knows Bharatanatyam, the classical dance style, and she is teaching it to me in return for German lessons. She is a most ingenious sculptor, too, and has constructed an intricate, graceful, clever, and elaborate sculpture of an Indian wedding procession—made entirely out of her own toenail clippings. You'd have to see it to believe it, but it is really very beautiful, rather like stylized ivory—and after all, why should an elephant's calcium be better than our very own?

There was a party here, and the girl giving it gave me the very best fruit, a sort of bitter orange, but she and her friends only ate the ordinary fruit, the cheap kind. They were unwilling to let me taste it ('Only Indian people like it') and then I discovered that it was the most delicious kind of mango, that grows wild here. It reminded me of the time in Mexico City when everyone insisted on showing off the Insurance Building, but no one wanted to show us the ancient pyramids. I set them straight, and now I am bombarded with mangoes. At the party we also had something that tasted very much like stuffed potato, with curry, and I discovered that it was, in fact, stuffed potato with curry. They also have blintzes, which are called 'chapatis'.

A Bengali pun: tea (which is served constantly from 5 am, at which time I am awakened with a cup of it, until 10 pm, when it serves as a nightcap) is called *cha*, and the word for servant, from the Sanskrit, is *chaakar* [which basically means 'one who works' but could be broken up to mean 'one who makes tea']. The Bengalis insist that this is ancient proof of the fact that the servants do nothing but make tea all day.

It's funny, but when I first came here I thought I would be good at being Indian because I was convinced I knew so much about India, and to a certain extent that's true. But I didn't count on the gulf created by what they *don't* know, about Lincoln and Robert Frost and Jones Beach. I think it is what we *are* that makes the distance between people, not what we are not.

9. *September 11, 1963,*
Shantiniketan

The last few days have been extremely humid and hot, not like anything I have ever known at home. Perhaps a steam bath, or a freak day in the noon sun at Jones Beach, could approximate what it is like in the shade here, but there, there is always relief, in the water or an air-conditioned room or when the sun goes down, but here it goes on and on day and night until even the Indians go and lie down and complain to each other. The sweat soaks through your clothes and actually drips from you, forming a little pool beside you, and you can feel your pulse in your forehead. The back of your throat stings the way it does when you get water up your nose, and your hands tremble when you lift them. Nobody moves much, and nobody eats very much, and no work is done. September is not usually this bad, but the monsoon has not been good this year, and the rains don't come every day to cool the air. But last night when everyone was at their wits' end, the storm finally came, after a week that made a New York heat wave seem like an early frost. All during the evening the air was completely, unnaturally still and close, and the electricity failed so there were no fans to keep the air moving (every room in India has a ceiling fan about five feet in diameter that turns constantly, so that it is always very difficult to light a cigarette, and every paper must be weighted down, but the electricity fails pretty often, and we have no fans in our bedrooms anyway), and the air really seemed to stick in your ears and nose and eyes like a fuzzy blanket, so that sounds were muffled and shapes blurred. Then the sky filled with lightning, but no thunder, just bursts of light, filling the whole sky with a brilliant blue light like the light of a big blue bomb, and in the middle a streak of yellow lightning that darted out not all at once but starting from one point and stretching out into a line, as if it were being drawn by an invisible pencil. And then, after several hours of this, great claps of thunder like the snapping of a celestial whip, and sudden gusts of wind that made all the shutters crash closed, and finally a downpour so thick that when you looked out through it, in the bursts of lightning that made it bright as day, the shapes of the trees in the yard were distorted as shapes are bent under water. And it was marvellously cool, and everybody woke up and ran around closing windows, and the children woke up and sang (because there was no electricity and the children always sing when the lights go out, partly because they're afraid, and partly because it's a great joke here), and finally when it let up, around five in the morning, we all went back to sleep and the birds took over our watch. Now there are pools everywhere, and the lizards and snakes are gambolling about in the paddy fields.

Random notes: I saw an Indian movie called *Cobra Girl*. It was a really terrible movie, sort of an Indian impression of Hollywood's impression of India, with pasteboard sets out of the old DeMille days, and tasteless sequined costumes, and special effects that didn't come off at all (a magician makes the heroine tiny, and the superimposed figure is surrounded with a funny light, and the people who are supposed to be looking at her look in the wrong place, etc.), and a lot of singing with the voices dubbed in completely wrong, and, finally, as a grand finale, when the hero and villain are fighting in the sky, the sound track burst into a recording of Tchaikovsky's 1812 Overture, Marseillaise and all. But there was a terrific fight between a wolf and a leopard, and between a snake and an alligator, and a good time was had by all. Last night they showed a very old Tarzan picture which seemed as sophisticated as the theatre of the absurd, after *Cobra Girl.*

I went to a lovely ceremony yesterday, where a six-month-old baby took her first solid food. She was dressed in a tiny sari, and her face was painted with flowers and jewels, and everyone was very jolly. In a few weeks I am going to go to a wedding, and even have a chance to help dress and paint the bride, as she is a good friend of my friend Chanchal. I must tell you more about her.

Chanchal would be the person to have with you on a desert island. She is very clever, and very jolly, and thinks she is very wicked (because she talks to boys, and because her friend that is getting married was already secretly married a month ago, and Chanchal helped them elope, and also because she knows dirty jokes, which she tells with great glee, the kind [my twelve-year-old brother] Tony tells. Sample: 'What did one mouse say to the other mouse? Come around the corner and I'll show you my hole') and she has a terrific temper: the other day at the post office she staged a fight worthy of the heroes of the *Mahabharata* [the great ancient Sanskrit poem about a fratricidal war]. The man at the window asked her to put water on the stamps instead of spitting on them, but the water was a good distance away, and Chanchal will never take a step more than she has to, so she burst out: 'You think you can insult me not to spit? I am furious. What to do? I am going to spit every one of these stamps. I am going to spit them right under your nose.' And she did, too. We are not allowed to have fans in our room: she has a fan, and an electric stove, too. She is always giving me things to eat ('Everyone knows that Punjabi food is the best food in India,' she says, in her Punjabi accent). She is very learned, knows all sorts of great stories (she is working on a PhD in vernacular folk stories) and still insists that homeopathic medicine is the only thing that works. She has big round eyes and beautiful tiny teeth like a child's teeth, and she brushes them with peroxide every day, 'for keeping white'. Literate and mature, she is delightfully Indian. I gave her the acid test yesterday. We had been talking about going to the famous temple of the sun at Konark, and then to the seaside resort of Puri nearby. That night I dreamed that my whole family and my fiancé had come to India to visit me, and Daddy was sulking because my fiancé and I were going to share a room, and so I went up to Daddy and told him that I would take him to Konark and Puri to make up for it, and not take my fiancé. Now, I figured there was a dream that any kindergartener in America could figure out. I told it to Chanchal, and asked her what she thought, and she said, in all seriousness, 'I guess you certainly think about Konark and Puri all the time.' So she is my friend for life, because that's what *I* consider the significance of the dream, too.

More random notes: There is an enormous statue in front of our hostel, a life-sized cast of three enormous cows with fish tails. I asked what the significance was, hoping for some new avatar or perhaps a theriomorphic folk deity, and was told that the sculptor had originally planned to have three mermaids, but the authorities said that mermaids were immodest to have in front of a woman's hostel, so he made them into mer-cows, because cows are always a safe bet.

Dogs in Bengali are said to bark 'Gheu geur'. Someday I'm going to compile a list of the different onomatopoeic representations of animal sounds.

Thank you for feeding me whole wheat bread so that I am the only American in history to remain healthy during the Indian monsoon, and for educating me and inspiring me with *A Passage to India* so that I wanted to come here, and for sending me to Radcliffe, and for letting me study Sanskrit in the days when no one in Great Neck knew whether it was a vegetable or an Egyptian king, and for letting me go away for a year without worrying about me.

10. September 15, 1963,
Shantiniketan

Now autumn has begun to set in. Everywhere the fields are filled with *kash*, which is a kind of feathery white flower, shaped like wheat, but made of the fuzzy stuff that flies in the air when dandelions go to seed, but silkier. *Kash* is to autumn here what the turning of leaves is to autumn there. It still rains every day, but only for a short time, and the ground is dry again in an hour, though the sun is not very hot. I went to Bolpur to buy some saris and a round of sulfaguanidine and enterovioform for the boys in the back room [a line from an old Marlene Dietrich song], and it was market day. The road was filled with pregnant goats and tiny fuzzy calves and sadhus looking very saintly and beautiful in their long white hair and beards. Near a store there was a woman crouching on the ground, crying in a weeping, rhythmic way, and there was a circle of children around her. I found out that the man in the shop said that she had tried to steal rice, and he had beaten her. She said that she had paid him, but she didn't say it with much conviction. We bought some rice and put it in her bowl, but she kept on moaning softly. Usually I am afraid to give money to the beggars; I can't explain why. They chant from a distance, and the sound gets closer and closer, and takes on a remote resemblance to the religious chant it is supposed to be, and then you hear the footsteps, and suddenly you see a face right at your window, a thin, scarred, discoloured face with wrinkles that are almost like folds, and a hand is thrust in between the wrought iron latticework of the window, and the voice is as rhythmic and whining as the sound a chicken makes. The first time anyone came to my window I actually ran away; now I give once a week to quiet my conscience a little, and then whenever I hear that droning sound, I take my book and go to a room that has no outside window, and I hear the sound coming to my window, and waiting there, and then it goes away, and I return to my desk. This happens perhaps twice a day.

Well, we went on to Bolpur. The huts there are covered with thatch, and on the walls there are hundreds of neat round paddies of cow dung, which they put on the walls to dry and then use for fuel. (My food is all cooked over cow dung, and it all tastes like cow dung to me. I know it's all in my mind, but it really does taste sort of smoked, especially the bland foods, and not smoked with just anything.) It used to give me quite a start to see a little girl of three or four, carrying a little bowl under her arm, suddenly run to pick something up, and I would think she had found a stone or a plant or something, and then she would stoop and eagerly put her hand into a great wet cow flop, and scoop up several handfuls and put them into her bowl with great gusto, and then go on looking for more. Then she would make it into mud pies and paste it on the sides of the house to dry. I've gotten used to seeing it now, but it does spoil my appetite for an hour or two.

On the side of one of these clay, thatched huts I saw a bas relief of a horse, in stature and stance somewhat resembling the T'ang horses at gallop, and in style something like the Picasso bulls, altogether one of the most beautiful things I've ever seen, and about eight feet long.[*] I keep meaning to take a photograph of it, but I never carry my camera here because it's home to me. Sometimes I see little white boys, but completely white, albinos with

---

[*] This description of the horse on the thatched hut finally made it into my book *Winged Stallions and Wicked Mares*, in 2021.

white hair and skin, playing with the Santhals, who are very dark, but they are purely hereditary accidents; there is almost no intermarriage with white-skinned people among the Santhals.

It is difficult to shop in Bolpur, because the stores open for half an hour, then close for two hours, then open for fifteen minutes, then close again, and so on, and as each shop has its own schedule, and as no one has a watch anyway, and as store hours (as well as the hours of classes at Shantiniketan, by the way) change every week or so as the hours of sunlight change, it is very confusing. Moreover, the store closes when anyone dies, and as someone is always dead, it is hard to find a time when you can buy several different things. Things at Shantiniketan are casual, too. Yesterday it looked like a fine day (here a fine day is a cloudy day; a clear day, the kind that we would call fine, is too hot to be fine) and so the students went to the vice chancellor and asked for a holiday, and he agreed, and so everyone went on a five-mile hike to the river, and pushed each other in, and then came back, getting thoroughly drenched by the rain on the way, and had afternoon classes. It's called an 'outing', and the students are allowed ten per year, whenever they want. The teachers come too, or else they go home and have tea.

I have not yet begun my Sanskrit classes, because my professor was supposed to arrive last week, but last week was the dark half of an inauspicious month, so he has to wait until the end of next week to come here, and meanwhile I am doing my research by myself, and getting along very well, inauspicious month or no. (I am temporarily studying with another pandit.)

I was asking about the winter here, trying to find out if I needed more warm clothes, and nobody seemed able to tell me how cold it would get. Finally, Chanchal said, 'You know, Wendy, to tell the truth, after living through the heat each year I always forget what the winter is like.'

I have had to give up eating mangoes (though I love them dearly and was accustomed to having several at every meal), because they aren't good during the monsoon (like oysters in 'r-less' months) and they make you sick. They made me sick, but it was worth it, and now I am all better.

I went to a Hindu temple service in the village here. At the appointed time everyone (about ten people) rings a bell or bangs on a brass bowl or blows on a conch shell (which sounds like the shofer or chauffeur or however you spell it that you blow on Yom Kippur), and generally makes a terrible racket for about five minutes, during which the lizards all come out to see what's up, and the children run around and are slapped by their mothers, and the sadhus go on chanting, looking up angrily now and then to quiet the children (though how the noise can make any difference in that terrible bedlam is more than I could see; I think they just want to see if anyone is watching them chant), and then the priest of the temple throws a lot of water and flowers at the statues of the gods (a combination of Vishnu, Kali, and the Bengali snake goddess, enough to warm the heart of any ethical culturist, or Unitarian, or syncretist in the neighbourhood) and then throws some more at the people, and then he sets down a flaming incense burner, and everyone runs their fingers through it the way we used to dare each other to do with a candle flame, and then they sort of wash their faces with the smoke, or make the gesture of doing so, and the priest chants in a monotone exactly like Cardinal Cushing [Archbishop of Boston], so that all you can make out is an occasional 'with thee' or 'Jesus' (in their Bengali equivalents, of course), and then suddenly the noise stops, and everyone throws himself down on his hands and knees and face, and the priest sprinkles them, and it is all over. Then everyone is given a kind of candy made of milk, which is very sacred; the Bengalis say it is god, but I think they just like an excuse for candy (they eat it all the time, and are famous for their sweet teeth).

Then we drove home, smelling the particular smell of India that is compounded of incense, sweat, flowers, dust, cow dung, sour milk, melted butter, rain, grass, and wet earth. When I got home I took a new cake of soap, and it was from the Montauk Manor, and never was any piece of soap so incongruous; as I looked at it I thought of, and *felt*, the posh dining rooms, and the big bathrooms, and the hot water, and the band music, and as India was so strong around me, I really felt very strange indeed.

Yesterday we walked down to the canal after a heavy rain. We hopped on a bullock cart for the last mile or so. 'I'm not tired of walking,' I said, thinking that Chanchal had suggested the cart because of her American friend, whose sandals were soaked through and coming off at every step. Chanchal looked very shocked and serious. 'It is for great enjoyment that we ride on bullock carts,' she said. And it was.

The ground by the canal is very red and mostly clay, and the grass grows in clumps something like the grass on sand dunes. The wind is gentle but constant, and everything sounds very far away. The Bengal countryside is flat and green, and after the rain we could see for miles, but beside the canal there is a high bank, which forms the horizon for several miles, until it meets a little jungle grove. Along the canal, below the high bank, a herd of cows were grazing, and there were some goats and dogs and scrawny chickens mixed in with them; and a few tiny little boys with bamboo sticks and no clothing were running in and out among the cows, supposedly tending them. And while we looked at them, and they looked at us, I heard the sound of a kind of flute playing a lively but sad song. And I turned and saw the strangest little procession walking along the bank above us, silhouetted against the dark grey sky with that special shimmering halo that bright objects have in a summer storm. They were little boys, about ten of them, coming home from school, all dressed in white dhotis, barefooted, one or two of them carrying black umbrellas open against the sun (which broke hotly through the clouds) and walking single file along the narrow bank, with several yards between each one and the next. The little round spots of their heads, and their skinny arms and legs coming out of their white dhotis, made them look like stick figures, or children's drawings, and with the umbrellas they looked like animated dotted 'i's. One of them must have been playing the flute that I heard, although I couldn't see anyone playing, and no one said a word, but they were all dancing a sort of shuffling, leaping polka, and they kept dancing until we lost sight of them, and could only hear the flute. Then the little boys who had been watching them

with us went back to playing with the cows, and we hailed
a bullock cart and went home to tea.

I have discovered one of the reasons why I so love
Indian myths: they are all glorified shaggy dog stories. Here
is one of the shaggiest. I just came across it, and I don't
think it has ever been translated.[*]

Once upon a time, Diti gave birth to a race of demons,
and they were all killed in a battle with the gods, whose
leader was Indra. Diti performed asceticism for thousands
of years and was granted the boon that she would bring
forth a child who would slay Indra. She carried the embryo
in her womb for twelve years, and all during this time
Indra kept bringing her flowers and presents of one sort
or another. Finally, she said, 'I'm pleased with you, my
son (I forgot to tell you, Indra was her son), and because
you've been so nice, I promise you that the child I bear
will *not* be an Indra-slayer.' Indra said that made him very
happy, and then he went away. As the sun had reached the
middle of the sky, Diti went to sleep, sitting down with
her knees up, which is an impure position. Indra came and
saw her asleep, and seeing the space exposed, he entered
her womb, took out his thunderbolt (Indra is Zeus), and
cut the foetus into seven pieces. Then he came out again,
and Diti woke up. When she learned what he had done,
she was very angry, but then he said, 'You were sleeping in

---

[*] I was wrong about that; it had been translated several times. I also got
several details quite wrong in this rendition, but I got them right in the
books and articles that I went on to write about the story, beginning with
Hindu Myths (1975) and most recently in 'Wars Within the Womb, in
Classical Hindu Mythology' (2022).

an impure position, and anyway it is not a sin to kill one's enemy.' And she said, 'You're right, Indra. I guess it was my fault. So I am not going to curse you.' And she didn't. And that's the story. And you can talk until you're blue in the face about Freud, and the phallic thunderbolt, and the prevalence of incest in creation myths, and the contrast between ritualistic and warrior ethics in a transitional society, and the return to the womb, until you drop, but *I* say that's a shaggy dog story.

Yesterday an American linguistics professor from Michigan came to lecture here, and I liked him right off, and I don't usually like the Americans who come to visit and stay here (I'm jealous of my position as the only American at Shantiniketan, I guess, and most of the Americans in India are really pretty awful), and I couldn't figure out what it was that made me feel so at home with him. And then when we were talking about not minding the Indian traditional restrictions as long as they didn't happen to restrict our own particular vices, he said it was like the Talmudic saying that it depended on whose bull was being gored,[*] and then I knew why I liked him—a New York Jew.

My Sanskrit pandit takes snuff, which I had never seen done before, and I find that it is traditional for Sanskrit pandits to take snuff. Tagore even wrote a poem about it: 'In the quarter where the Sanskrit pandits live, the snuff rises and covers the sky. The pandits are engaged

---

[*] A line, more often cited as 'whose ox is being gored', often said to be based on Exodus 21:28–36, about legal culpability for an ox that gores a person or another animal, but more probably derived from Martin Luther, in the 1521 Diet of Worms: 'Most human affairs come down to depending on whose ox is gored.'

in a subtle argument: is the pot a container of oil, or is the oil contained in the pot?' This may be too Bengali for you to appreciate, but I love it. And, as they say, it loses in translation. My pandit keeps his snuff in a snail shell which is sealed with lac, which is very pretty, but it gets all over everything, and the total effect is enough to make the Sanskrit room worse than the Duchess's kitchen with its pepper ('Wah, wah, wah' and all that...) [in *Alice in Wonderland*].

11. September 18, 1963, Shantiniketan

I think I know one of the reasons why everything in Bengal looks so magnificently beautiful. There is something unique and queer about the light. To begin with, everything is green, different shades of green ranging from forest green (in the forests, of course) to a bright goldy green that I have never seen anywhere else. And the air is warm and moist, so that everything looks very far away and blurry, and story-bookish, something like the backgrounds in Renaissance portraits. And it is so completely flat that there is really just one low horizon. This is the background, and then, in this hazy, flat, hypnotic green, objects appear in the foreground, highlighted by a sudden shaft of light that breaks through the clouds (here there are millions of thick, tiny, fast-moving clouds, so that it is truly sun-shower and rainbow territory) and silhouetted against the flat horizon, and the only colour other than green, and the total effect is such that the object in the foreground leaps out at you like the figures in a 3-D lens viewer, or the glowing images that appear when a figure is superimposed in colour movies, or spotlighted on a dim stage. And so your eyes are fascinated by whatever you are looking at, a flower or a cow or a tree, and it looks magical (perhaps I feel it as magical because I am so reminded of the superimposed figures in films, and those are usually magical figures, Superman flying through the sky or the Good Witch of the North [in *The Wizard of Oz*] suddenly appearing), and very precious, like the single vase in a Japanese room. Perhaps this is what gave such a magical aura to the line of dancing boys I saw last week; the objects in the landscape seem to be in another dimension; their details are terribly sharp, surprisingly sharp, like the things you suddenly see through field glasses, and all the more so because of the exquisite softness of the background landscape, which looks as if it were photographed through gauze. You really expect them to disappear the minute you turn away. Like Pindar's description of the Greek countryside: here there are more gods than men.

There was a festival yesterday, as there always seems to be for one reason or another, and part of the celebration was a swimming meet. In case you've forgotten what a swimming meet is like, let me remind you. You find a beautiful-looking pond in the middle of a bamboo grove (I say beautiful-*looking* not to be redundant, but because I learned, after expressing a desire to plunge in, that the lepers perform their toilette there), and everyone puts on his whitest dhoti or her brightest sari, rings in the nose, bells on the toes (really),[*] and stands around the pond

---

* Tripping on the line from the nursery rhyme 'Ride A Cock Horse To Banbury Cross': 'Rings on her fingers, bells on her toes'.

under the trees or under an umbrella. Then three men in
white turbans and loincloths get on three little rafts and
propel them, by long bamboo poles (bamboo poles are the
two-by-fours of India; everywhere you see scaffolds made
of bamboo lashed together), into the middle of the pond.
On the rafts are piles of shocking-pink-painted inner tubes.
Then eight girls in saris get into the water, saris and all,
and stand there looking foolish. Then someone says, '*Ek,
Dui, Tin,* [One, Two, Three] Go!' and they begin to splash
across. After a few minutes, in which it becomes apparent
that only one of the girls has any idea how to swim (which
is not surprising, since Indian women would have to swim
in saris, and so they don't, although the tribal women and
sweepers bathe in the river every day, combining a swim,
a shower, and a laundry job), the men on the rafts throw
one of the pink tubes to each of the girls, and the one girl
who manages to get across (the whole pond is perhaps
twenty yards in diameter) gets the prize (which is a garland
of jasmine and hibiscus and lots of things I don't know
the name of) and everyone cheers, and then they sing the
Indian national anthem, and then they go on a picnic. And
that's the swimming meet. On the picnic, the food is served
on banana leaves instead of plates, and you drink tea out
of little clay cups that are then thrown away, as the earth
is made of clay here. All in all, it was the most wonderful
swimming meet I have ever seen.

Last night the Santhals (very beautiful tribal people of
Bengal. They earn about a dime a day, out of which they
spend seven cents on toddy, according to the Bengalis. The
women carry their children under their saris like papooses,

and have beautiful breasts, and carry jugs on their heads, and look very majestic and angry) were having a festival, and I wanted to go, and everyone said, 'Oh, you don't want to see that. They just get drunk and dance,' and so of course then I was *dying* to see it, and finally I went out in a terrific rain to go to the village, but then the drums stopped, so we knew it must be over. But there will be one next week, and I will see that. Since we were out in the rain, we stayed out, and sang songs and ran around barefoot and came back and had tea.

I have found the perfect description of my linguistic shortcomings. It's from Pope: 'He has too little Latin. He finds the Latin from the meaning, not the meaning from the Latin.'* Well, I have always been that way about Sanskrit, but I am finally learning the language the right way; the pandit here is teaching me grammar and philology, and I love it.

One of the things that I miss here is the feeling of being in an exotic place, which I expected to have. But I am so very much at home here—the climate, the landscape, even the languages are so familiar, and Rubi and Puri (the two women servants here) take such good care of me, making me tea, and fixing the folds on my sari, and carefully wringing out my drip-dry dresses, that I actually have the feeling that I will have to travel—to Benares or Cape Comorin or Darjeeling—to find an exotic place.

---

* I have not been able to locate this quote in the writings of Alexander Pope, or indeed anywhere else. We also used to refer to this level of knowledge of a classical language as having 'Loeb Latin' or 'Loeb Greek', from the Loeb Library publications that had the Latin or Greek on one page and the English translation on the other.

Outside my window is a tree which puts out a new white flower every morning. By noon the flower is a lovely soft pink; by evening it is crimson, and by night it dies.

Some Lebanese men who spoke only French came to visit, and I spoke French with them, and I was amazed to find how much my French had been improved by the last month's practice in expressing myself in a foreign language, even though that language wasn't French. I guess most of it is a matter of attitude after all.

For years Bengali children have been learning to read with three little books written by Tagore, and I am using them, and they're the most beautiful poetry, and very cleverly designed to highlight the particular linguistic problems that Bengali poses. I have learned a few Bengali songs, and they just love to hear me sing them; it gives them a tremendous kick, and they are always bringing their friends to hear me sing. And then they teach me more songs.

I saw a bullock cart loaded with blankets and chairs, carrying someone's entire belongings to a new house. I wonder how many bullock carts it would take for us to move.

12. September 22, 1963,
Shantiniketan

I can't get used to the terrific contradictions in the Indian attitudes towards sex. The *Kama Sutra* tells all sorts of subtle ways to choose a woman who will be good in bed, but no one gets a chance to choose a woman at all. Khajuraho stands there in plain sight, making everyone who sees it

get hot all over, but the Indian newspapers are just now
making a great fuss over the fact that now for the first
time the hero and heroine in an Indian movie are to be
allowed to kiss (and a very chaste kiss it is, too, none of
your writhing and drooling for them, no sir). Everywhere
men and women [considered 'lower' caste in the Hindu
hierarchy] walk around naked and no one gives them a
second glance, but the ['upper'-caste] Hindu women must
cover up every inch of skin except for their hands and
heads, even in terrible heat, even when they bathe or sleep.
(This last paradox makes sense, I guess, in terms of caste:
because the outcastes [people once called Untouchables
and now called Dalits] are forced by their circumstances
to walk around naked, so the [higher-caste] Hindus must
do the opposite.)

And at Shantiniketan too: the rules are terribly strict
about talking to boys, and you couldn't if you wanted to,
because men and women are segregated everywhere, but
somehow people seem to elope all the time. To prevent
this, the rules are constantly being made more strict, but
this does not have the desired effect. For instance, they
made a rule that every girl must have a local guardian,
and he is the only man to whom she may talk. Well, one
girl just put down the name of her boyfriend as her local
guardian, and he guarded her as well as you might imagine.

Another thing that never fails to impress me is the
difference in standards of beauty. I see many girls here
of an exquisite beauty quite unlike anything I have ever
seen in American girls, but they are not the girls that the
Bengalis consider beautiful. There is one who looks like a

combination of Elizabeth Taylor and the girl in *The Cranes are Flying*,* and she is considered quite homely, because her skin is fairly dark. Another girl is dark, and quite Indian, but has pale green eyes, and the effect is quite startling. She too is considered quite homely. And it seems funny, because beautiful women, women who know that they are considered beautiful, that is, have a special way of behaving, and none of these girls have that at all, so that you almost miss them, and then when you chance to see their faces it is with a feeling almost of serendipity.

I have become quite friendly with the insects and lizards. They are big enough to have real personalities (the grasshoppers are about six inches long, the roaches the size of eggs, the lizards a foot long and very fat!†), and they pop out at you every time you open a drawer or close a shutter or move a chair. The lizards are very good company; they sit on the wall and the ceiling and run around looking anxious if you tickle them. I almost stepped on a snake yesterday, not a poisonous one but no darling either, and I'm afraid my burgeoning reptilian friendship does not apply to snakes. The crows are very nice, but they are enormous, and they fly into the rooms and try to pick up the shiny things, spoons and watches, and they knock things over and make a terrible racket. There is a bush right by my window that has flowers like little tiny rubber gloves, sort of, and a little bird whose beak is shaped

---

* A Russian film from 1957 starring the exquisitely beautiful Tatiana Samoilova.

† Here I wildly exaggerated the sizes of the beasts in question, for effect, as seems to have been a habit with me back then.

just right for the flowers comes every day with his friends and hops around and has dinner and sings and looks very beautiful. I give him pieces of bread.

I have discovered why Bengalis talk so very fast. They have to, to finish what they must say. They never mention gender or number, and usually leave out tense, too, but every time they mention something they have to state, with a fairly long affix, whether its shape is basically long and thin or flat, whether it is nice or not so nice, and whether there are a group of them. All of this takes time (you also have to say whether it is coming or going) and so you have to talk fast. It's interesting to see the difference between what they think is important and what I think is: this is true about living, too. They don't care at all about time (attention spans are infinite, and everyone is late) or possessions, but they care a lot about their own provinces and music and flowers.

America is front-page news here every day. Kennedy's speeches are reported, and commended; we've won the Cold War in Calcutta, it seems, especially now that the Russians are disturbing the market in Tibet; the old story of whose bull is gored... But also every day there is a photograph on the front page, showing a bombed church in Alabama, or a riot. The story of the white man who made a Black man swallow a snake got a terrific playup here (perhaps they liked it particularly because snakes are such a big thing here), but still no one has accused me or even questioned me about that. They are silent out of tact, I fear, because Chanchal certainly knows all about the treatment of Blacks in America, but still they don't seem to take it personally. For one thing, Indians can't make up their minds as to whether or not they are considered Blacks. The girl from Trinidad here has a terrific thing about colour,* even though she is Indian by birth, and yet the ones who have been to America, or who have friends who have been, seem to have been only in the north, and not discriminated against. But some of them have had trouble. It is a tricky business, and at first I had to be very careful not to tread on any toes, as I am the only white person here. At first the servants called me Memsahib, but now they call me Didi, which is what they call all the girls (sister), so I suppose I'm okay.

What music am I going to hear next month in Calcutta? Ravi Shankar? No. Duke Ellington.† Talk about carrying coals to Newcastle, this Mohammed is going to the mountain, and there's a mixed metaphor to put in your pipe and smoke.

They showed [the film] *Moby Dick* here, and the audience was really disturbed by the blood of the whale. They were impressed by the whale, though, and by Queequeg. I felt funny, knowing that of the hundreds of people watching the film, I was almost certainly the only one who had been to Nantucket, or who knew anything about that whole way of whaling.

I now have an army of little boys to practise my Bengali on. Whenever I meet them they say, 'Good morning. Give me a stamp. Do you have any little brothers at home

* This was a sarcastic euphemism for racial bigotry.

† I never wrote another word about this concert; perhaps I never attended it after all.

like me?' and like that. The children here live in a little
dormitory next door, and the conditions are awful. They
are very young—four and five, some of them—and there is
only one very deaf old lady to take charge of about sixty of
them, and they all live together in a few little rooms, and
whenever one of them gets sick they all get it, and they get
sick all the time because they eat nothing but rice; I don't
know if their parents know or not. I know that people
in India will sacrifice anything to get an education, and
perhaps this is the only way. But they are awfully young to
be on their own like that. There is a wonderful song that
they sing, 'We are a train going faster and faster', something
like *The Little Engine That Could*,[*] and it gets higher and
higher, and they shout the high notes, and they sing it all
the time, and laugh and laugh.

It has become known to the general populace that I
love cats, and every time one appears they shout, 'Pushycat,
pushycat' (Bengalis have no dental 's', only a palatal 's'),
which is to alert me.

There are a lot of Bengali jokes about Sikhs. One tells
of the Sikh who, walking with Queen Elizabeth by a river
in England, told her that she had lovely buttocks (*botok*
is the Hindi for 'swan'); another, of the Sikh who, caught
at a friend's house one night when the monsoon came,
and invited to spend the night there, disappeared and

---

[*] One of my favourite children's books. Going up a steep hill, the little
engine said to himself, 'I think I can, I think I can,' slower and slower as
he approached the top, and then he went over the top and said, 'I thought
I could, I thought I could,' faster and faster as he went down the other
side of the hill.

returned, drenched, telling that he had gone home to get his nightshirt.

More about Chanchal. Last night she insisted upon eating two chilis (a kind of pickled pepper so hot that even the Indians take only a tiny piece with their rice), and after howling and drinking great quantities of water and sugar (she drinks by holding the bottle a foot over her mouth, pouring it in and swallowing that way. Try it some time, head back and all. It's impossible), she finally calmed down. 'Chanchal,' I said, 'why do you eat chilis if they do that to you?' 'I get such a terrific kick out of it,' she said. 'Oof, what to say?'

Last night we stayed up telling stories. I palmed off all my old jokes that you are so sick of hearing, much to Chanchal's delighted oofs and squeals, and I tried to explain Jewish logic, and then Chanchal told me about her childhood in Punjab. She lived in Lahore, and she was a tomboy, running around with her brother, stealing butter and then smoothing it out, stealing the cream of buffalo milk ('Ooof, buffalo cream is so sweet'), and sleeping in her father's bed ('Sometimes he would put me in another bed and put a pillow beside me to fool me, but I would know that the pillow wasn't him, and I would come right back to his bed again'). Although they were supposed to be vegetarians (her father was a Sikh, and very hotheaded and nervous), her mother would always cook meat for Chanchal (like Daddy's mother sneaking him milk in the kosher kitchen*). At night her mother would bring her a

---

* My father grew up in a small village in Poland, where his father kept a strictly kosher house. But his mother felt that a child should have milk

glass of milk ('Buffalo milk, of course. Cow's milk is just for babies and sick people. A normal person drinking cow's milk—oof!') and would have to sit by her bed until Chanchal finished it.

They lived in a joint family, with all the brothers' families, and the grandmother. What a grandmother! She was terribly religious and would have to bathe every time her shadow crossed the shadow of an outcaste, which happened about twenty times a day, as outcastes did the sweeping and washing. She also kept everyone out of her kitchen, to keep it pure, and no one could touch her clothes. When Chanchal wanted to tease her, she would run into the kitchen and touch the clothes, and the grandmother would have to wash everything completely. Everything would make her impure, and she would go into the bathroom, running the tap full force, and mutter curses into it so that no one could hear her.

When Partition came, they left, but they expected to come back again; they never thought that the trouble would last as it did, and so they left everything there. They handed the house over to the Mussalmans [Chanchal used the usual Hindustani word for Muslims], and the grandmother cleaned the kitchen with water from the Ganges and locked it and said to the head of the Mussalmans, 'Please, you can go in the whole house, but please, please stay out of my kitchen.' And they never saw the house again. Chanchal was seven years old, and she remembers the things she

---

with every meal, and so even when there was a meal with meat, at which Jewish law prohibits milk, she would call my father out to the kitchen on some pretext and silently give him a glass of milk to drink.

saw very distinctly: four Hindu boys ('very young, they did not know how to kill properly') attacked a Mussalman and tried to kill him, and they kept cutting at him, and he cried out, but they couldn't kill him, and then they dragged him to drown him in the canal, but there was no water in the canal, and he kept on screaming, and finally they threw a boulder on him. And Chanchal watched this. Then the boy who had killed him had to flee from the Mussalman police, and Chanchal's mother hid him, and gave him fresh clothes, as his were drenched in blood. He slept there that night, but the next day he ran away, and they killed him. And Chanchal saw a house set on fire, and the Mussalmans were throwing the Hindus into the fire, hurling them by the arms and legs. And many more things like that.

Well, then we went back to telling stories. We both love children's stories best of all (we confided in each other, because we both are studying children's stories, I in Sanskrit and she in Apabhramsa dialects, and we swapped many of these), and I told her all about *Alice in Wonderland* and *Mary Poppins*, and she told me about the tricks they used to play, and their stories. She doesn't like Bengali movies 'because the Bengalis only like tragedy and crying, and I only like daylight and laughing', and that is Chanchal in a nutshell, if you could find such a big nutshell.

13. September 27, 1963,
Shantiniketan

We were talking about Pakistan taking aid from both US and China, and Chanchal said, 'What, Pakistan wants to eat with both hands, is it?'

In India, parrots say, '*Namaste namaste namaste namaste namaste...*' which I suppose I should have expected, but still it struck me as terribly funny.

I have finally discovered the most useless phrase in any language. Useless knowledge here hath made her masterpiece. Chanchal was teaching me some Chinese words (she knows some Chinese) and one phrase she taught me was 'Poo ka chee', which means, 'Please don't be formal'. In Chinese, mind you. More useless than the former champion, 'I'm asleep'.

Did I say that Chanchal could supply you with anything? Well, I was feeling like not working yesterday (quite different from not feeling like working, you know), and Chanchal whipped out a copy of P.G. Wodehouse's *Laughing Gas*, her favourite book, and the best of all possible not-working tools. I thought I was eclectic, but she is crazy about Wodehouse and D.H. Lawrence but has never *heard* of Lewis Carroll or James Joyce.

Prostitution was outlawed several years ago in India, and all the newsreels have shots of the girls learning weaving and knitting in special reformation centres.

The beginning Bengali books I am reading are all about food. The children are always hungry, and this is the best way to keep their attention. Dick, Jane and Sally* are a luxury that only American children can afford.

For a while I thought that Indian erotic writings fell in the same category of vicarious release, but now I think

---

* The *dramatis personae* in the book (*Fun with Dick and Jane*) that children of my generation were first given as they learned to read. There was also a dog named Spot and a cat named Puff.

it is more than that. Indians find a strong tie between extreme chastity and extreme eroticism. (A minor example of this sort of thing in America is in the old movies where the buxom heroine wears a high, lacey blouse, erotic by contrast and suggestion.) There is a lot more to it in India, where monasticism and yoga have such a hold, but I have come to see it as two sides of the same coin, rather than a paradox at all. In the old myths, if a man wanted a son, he would become an ascetic for a thousand years, and if a woman wanted a husband, she would practise yoga. Then too, the men would store up virility by chastity (this is an old thing in America too, even in Frank Harris with his little string[*]), and innocence has always been the most important requirement of an Indian heroine, even more than in Europe.[†]

There is a tree here where all the littlest birds come every night at sunset, and they all sing at once, and it sounds like a flock of tiny bells ringing and ringing. The tree that changes its flowers from white to red now has some white and some red on it, and it reminds me of the gardeners in *Alice in Wonderland*, painting half the white roses red before the queen caught them.

I saw a performance of Kathakali dancing, and in the middle of it the dancer burst into a rhythmic utterance:

---

[*] Frank Harris's notorious autobiography, *My Life and Loves*, documented his sexual adventures, but I have absolutely no memory of what he did with string.

[†] These rather jumbled ideas became, in transformation, the central theme of my Harvard PhD dissertation, 'Asceticism and Eroticism in the Mythology of Siva' (1968), and my first book, *Siva: The Erotic Ascetic* (1973).

'*Da da rigidigi taragara ra digidigi ra ra...*'

All nonsense or real old scat.[*]

Last night there was a terrific rain, cooling everything off, knocking down blankets of flowers, making red mud everywhere, and delighting all the animals, especially the smaller ones. The dogs have come to life and are mating hot and heavy; they must read Sanskrit *kavyas* [poems], for the rains are the traditional season for it. They must also read the *Kama Sutra*, for some of them go at it back to back or ass to ass in a manner which I would not have thought possible.

I have had no mail for several days, because there was a strike for one day in Calcutta. They strike from time to time, as the price of rice has risen terribly and the wages have stayed the same, but they can only afford to strike for one day, as they have no savings. It's difficult to hold out for days when you live from hand to mouth. Last year there was a strike at Shantiniketan, protesting some new rules, and of course it was a hunger strike, and they won it.

During the Puja holidays the lights are left on and the door open so that owls might fly in by mistake; the goddess of fortune rides on an owl, and any time you see an owl she is there on him, but invisible. Every god rides on an animal, Shiva on a bull, Devi on a lion, Kama on a crocodile, and Ganesha, the elephant god, on a mouse,[†] of

---

[*] A kind of jazz singing invented by Louis Armstrong, improvised with wordless sounds or nonsense syllables.

[†] Actually a bandicoot, much bigger than a mouse, though still not big enough to carry an elephant, or even an elephant-headed god, which is what Ganesha is.

course. (He uses a whip, I guess, like the man who got a kitten to carry his piano upstairs.*)

People wander into my room all the time to look at me and practise their English, and sometimes when I am working, I am not the perfect host. Last night in the midst of some Sanskrit passage a girl wandered in and stood there, and I looked up from my work with a sort of, 'Well, what is it?' kind of look, but I didn't say anything, and she didn't say anything, and finally she smiled as if to humour me in my stupidity, and said, 'For nothing.' And I really felt one upped. People here really go straight to the point, and they always seem to know what the point really is.

I went to a movie about a dancing courtesan, and at the very beginning, where the lion roars or the sweaty man beats the gong in our pictures, there was a shot of the most delicate statue of a woman dancing with her skirt flaring at the bottom and her arms raised, turning slowly, a bit like the Degas dancing girls, but delicate as a fairy, and exquisitely carved. The movie itself was fascinating, with one strange scene in which a woman acts, in a play, the role of her rival in love, not knowing why the hero is so moved, thinking not of her but of the woman she is representing.† And in the middle of the stage, for absolutely

---

* Old Jewish joke. A man visited his friend in a fourth-floor walk-up apartment in Manhattan and saw that he had a concert grand piano there. 'Goodness,' he exclaimed, 'how did you ever get that piano up all those stairs?' 'Easy,' said his friend; 'the cat carried it up.' 'But how could a small cat carry up such a heavy piano?' 'Simple. We used a whip.'

† This was a theme that I was to develop in *The Woman Who Pretended to Be Who She Was* (2005) and in my translation of a Sanskrit play in which such a scene occurs, Harsha's *Priyadarshika*, in *The Lady of the Jewel Necklace and The Lady Who Shows Her Love* (2006).

no reason that I could discern, shining forth among the flashes of stage lightning and the singing and dancing, was a white cross with INRI clearly written above it.

A Swiss violinist gave a recital here last night, the first non-Indian music I have heard since I came here. He played a Bach sonata, and stood in a bare stage, with the back brick wall showing, and ladders lying about (for me it had all the associations of Pirandello [author of the 1921 play *Six Characters in Search of an Author*] and *Our Town* [Thornton Wilder's 1938 metatheatrical play]), but to the Indians of course it was an eyesore, there being no curtains or couches. I guess they didn't know what scenery to use for a Swiss violinist, and come to think of it, neither do I. At the first notes I felt such a tremendous surge of richness and familiarity, all the little motifs and patterns, and the velvet sound of the instrument itself, so different from the plaintive whine of the sitar or the pulse of the tabla. I don't think I have ever listened to music as I did then, hearing the whole of European civilization in the perfect balance and melody of that one violin on a skeletal stage in the tropical night, perfumed and restless. Chanchal had never heard a violin before and had never heard of Bach at all. I tried to explain it to her ahead of time, but what could you say about keys, and themes, and mathematics, and harmonies that would explain Bach? I was so afraid that she wouldn't like it, but she sat there with her knees up and her head down, and when it was over she was positively ecstatic. 'Soooooo sweet,' she said. 'How much there must be to practise to play so nice!' And the others liked it too, asking him to 'play us another song', but I think he was a bit

put off when, after [he] smilingly ask[ed] them what they
would like to hear, they asked for the Moonlight Sonata.

I was talking to Chanchal about going to Benares, and
she said, 'Oof, such a wicked city,' and I said I thought
it was a holy city, and she said, 'Yes, of course, holy and
wicked. Always it is like that with holy places. They have
the Ganges right there, and so they can go and do all their
sins and then just splash themselves a little and start right
in again.' Chanchal doesn't believe in the Hindu gods ('If
you are happy and you don't feel guilty about anything, that
is god,' she says), but then, 'I never like to hurt anyone's
feelings, so when I see Ram or Krishna I go up to him and
say, "*Namas te, Ram.*"' Her father was a pious Sikh but he
drank brandy and whiskey, and once Chanchal caused him
great embarrassment when, asked in nursery school what
the word 'neat' meant, she said, 'Without soda.' Chanchal
used to pretend to have a cold so that she would get some
brandy, and the little two-year-old nephew used to insist
upon a sip of 'vishi' too. Quite an indulgence, for Scotch
costs about $25 a bottle, but children are never denied
anything in India. When Chanchal's brother's child woke
up one morning screaming that he wanted a ring so that
he could marry his Mashi (aunt, i.e. Chanchal), his mother
went to the market and brought back a ring, and he gave
it to Chanchal, and then danced around her, shouting and
clapping his hands. And she still wears the ring. Chanchal
has never been to a dentist and has never worn shoes. She
is an accomplished palm-reader, so I figured I'd let her have
a go at mine. She stared at it and then said, 'I'm afraid I
can't read it properly. It says that you will marry and be

divorced at twenty-two, but you are twenty-two now.' So
I think there may be something in it after all [because she
was right]. She would never have just thought of a thing
like that.

14. October 1, 1963,
Shantiniketan

I have come across a Bengali saying that beats the Viennese
all hollow. It is a glorious, brief combination of 'Lieber sich
den Magen verrenken als dem Wirt etwas zu schenken'* and
'Wenn man dir gibt, nimm; wenn man dir nimmt, schrei'.† In
Bengali it goes: 'Oi jaay oi jaay Bangalir meye, khey jaay,
chey jaay, jaaye niye.' Literally: 'There goes, there goes,
Bengali's daughter. (She has) eaten, asked (for more), and
goes bringing (some away with her).' Talk about Indo-
Germanic unity of thought. But after all, nobody here but
us Aryans.‡

Last night the littlest boys put on a kind of door-to-door
show, and one little boy dressed up with a sari over his
head and did the most hilarious little dance, a combination
of an opera buffa transvestite, a middle-aged man trying
to learn the hula, Zero Mostel dancing, and the way little

---

* A Viennese saying. Roughly: 'Sooner let your stomach break / Than let
the waiter take your steak.'

† Another Viennese saying: 'When someone gives you something, take
it; when someone takes something from you, scream.' See *The Donigers of
Great Neck* for both of these sayings.

‡ A reference to an old joke, of which the punchline is, 'Nobody here
but us chickens', spoken by a fox hiding in the hen house, in reply to the
farmer who calls out, 'Who's there?' The implication is that it's just the
usual crowd. Nowadays I would say 'Indo-European' rather than 'Aryan'.

boys the world over imitate women. It was a true delight to behold, and he enjoyed it most of anyone.

'*Hindi Chini bhai bhai*' means 'Indians and Chinese are brothers', and it is what Chou En Lai said when he visited India some time ago. Now it is a general purpose sarcastic phrase, roughly equivalent to 'Your mother wears (Chinese Red) army boots' or 'Tell it to the Marines'.

Chanchal cooked a Punjabi meal for me. Now I can face the fire and brimstone undaunted on the day of reckoning; it is mere lemon sherbet compared to Punjabi food. Rice is the base,[*] and then it is sprinkled generously with spices and lightly with bits of meat and vegetables and fish. I think Indian cooking could be summed up in the following betel nutshell: they use spices the way we use food, and vice versa. After the first course I pleaded for mercy, and Chanchal gave me a kind of cool, sweet yogurt. I was delighted to find such sympathy for my blistered esophagus, but I had no sooner finished the yogurt when she said, 'Good, now you can start on the hot course refreshed. Like Romans!' I went to see the cook to get the chicken for the meal, and while I was there, storing up enough visual and olfactory memories to kill my appetite, he snatched up a scrawny, tiny chicken and tied its legs together, throwing it into a corner. I felt like a real heathen, and for a moment I understood why the Indians, who live among the animals, instead of picking up cellophane-wrapped packages at the market, would rather live on vegetables. Chanchal is not a strict vegetarian, but she won't eat steak. 'I don't eat big animals,' she says.

---

* Though wheat is the base of most Punjabi food.

Among a list of books by non-Indian authors about India, published in India (like Herman Hesse's *Siddhartha*, Edwin Arnold's *Light of Asia*, E.M. Forster's *Passage to India*), there appear Upton Sinclair's *The Jungle* and Machiavelli's *The Prince*.

15. *October 4, 1963,*
Shantiniketan

Last night a big black snake got into one of the bathrooms, and the poor *durwan* [porter, doorkeeper] was summoned and hit him on the head with a stick a few times; now the snake has gone down the toilet hole to die and is stopping up all the drains meanwhile. (There are a lot of Indian stories about magic serpents or lost treasure stopping up wells and things so that there is an investigation and then the denouement of the story. There's something like that in non-Indian folklore too, isn't there?) We are all anxiously waiting for the snake to die, like greedy heirs around a rich man's sickbed, and none of us more than the *durwan*, for he believes, as most of them do, that if the snake doesn't die, he will come out and find the man who injured him and kill him. It's not even a poisonous snake, but the *durwan* knows what he knows.

Yesterday was the birthday of Yubon, a Buddhist girl from Thailand, and to celebrate it she fed the Thai monks that live here, and she was really delighted by it, and very excited, because monks can take no food after noon each day, and lunch here is usually served, Indian-time-wise, sometime between eleven and one thirty, so she was afraid the food wouldn't come in time, but it did, and she fed them. She received presents, too—a gorgeous dress of heavy Thai silk and a terrycloth bathrobe from Japan, of which she of course preferred the latter—but the best part of her day was feeding the monks.

Chanchal wanted me to teach her her favourite American song, but she couldn't remember what it was, except that it was slow and about the moon. After making myself hoarse singing the first lines of every song I know, I discovered that it was 'You Are My Sunshine'.

You know how I have always rebelled against the para-spellings that make you say 'You need a [Uneida] biscuit' or 'Mighty [My Tea] fine' or some damn thing that you never knew you were saying until you heard the sounds come out of your own mouth? There really is something embarrassing and helpless about it, and it packs the same wallop as the kindergarten jokes that make you say, 'I 8 a monkey' or '[Adam and Eve and] Pinch me', realizing just a split second too late that you've fallen for it. Well, they have followed me to Bengal. There are many English words taken into Bengali, but distorted to fit the Bengali sound system, and transliterated into Bengali script. You come to a strange word, find that it isn't in the dictionary, and then go from the word in Bengali script to 'ishteshan' and then realize that it's 'station' (Bengalis can't pronounce an initial 'st' without a preceding vowel). To have gone to all that trouble just to discover that you were speaking your own language after all, all the time, is somehow insulting as well as irritating. And then, to say with relief, 'Oh, station!' only to be corrected, 'No, it's pronounced "ishteshan",' is enough to make a person switch to hieroglyphics or brail. And when you just begin to know when to brace yourself for a coming 'ishteshan', the language sneaks up behind you and starts rabbit punching you with '*kyepityen*' (captain), '*phutbol*' (football), '*biharar*' (bearer), '*torank*' (trunk) and the final blow, '*haromoniyam*' (harmonium). I suppose we owe them something in return for jungle, bungalow, dingy, bazaar and the other Bengali words we stole, but there must be an easier way to pay.

It still surprises me that in India, a country known for a rigid family organization, 'togetherness' with a vengeance extending to second cousins, and irrevocably arranged marriages, so many of the people I know here come from broken families.* Mishtuni's father, a famous translator, lives in Delhi where his work is, but her mother lives here taking care of her sick daughter. Chanchal's father is home only a few weeks in the year; the rest of the time he is away on business, some of it in Lahore where they used to live.† There are many women here at Shantiniketan who are living away from their husbands just so that they can get an education. Krishna, the girl who lives next door, has left her six-week-old baby with her grandmother and husband to come here.

16. *October 8, 1963,*
Shantiniketan

Yesterday I was in bed with a touch of the flu (called here the American flu, just as the English call syphilis the

---

* This was the wrong word, I think. I didn't mean divorced families, which 'broken families' usually implies, but families whom other circumstances had broken by forcing them to live apart from one another.

† I later learned, as the reader will (October 20, 1963), that there was a particular reason why Chanchal's father so seldom lived with Chanchal's mother.

French disease and the Spanish call it the Italian disease), really just a cold brought on by the crazy meanderings of the temperature during this change of seasons, but still a cold, making me feel all hot and tired and useless and motherless. Chanchal came in and straightened out the room for me and even brought me some roses from the garden outside. Here there are roses all year, and no one pays much attention to them; they are rather plain in comparison with all the flamboyant tropical flowers, but I am loyal and love them best, and they reminded me of our rose garden so staunchly defended against the battalions of squirrels, gardeners and small boys.

A little comedy unfolded about my bed. First of all, Chanchal insisted on getting me homeopathic medicines, and putting a Chinese balm on my head. Then they decided that the *real* doctor should come, and he turned out to be a beautiful white-haired man who felt my pulse with his thumb for about ten seconds, not looking at a watch because he didn't have one. He then announced that I just had a cold, and prescribed a kind of sulfa drug; I was debating whether or not to take it when I noticed that he was wearing a string of sandalwood beads around his neck and somehow something in me refused to swallow a pill prescribed by a man wearing sandalwood beads. So I didn't, and I got well anyway. I suppose Dr Katz[*] might wear beads if he were an Indian, and perhaps they are just the Indian equivalent of a Barlach collection, but I didn't want to mess around with sulfa.

---

[*] Dr George P.F. Katz, a German refugee and noted collector of Ernst Barlach sculptures, was our family doctor in Great Neck.

I was getting angry with the Indians [who wrote my Sanskrit texts] for being so careless and disorganized, making me go to such trouble in reading the Puranas because they insist upon telling every story from the middle, and then backing up on it by a series of rhetorical questions—Who was his father? How did his father come to be cursed? Who was the father of the sage who cursed him? Et cetera. And then I realized that the same disorderly quality of mind that was so infuriating in the Puranas was the very quality that could *think* of those crazy, fascinating stories in the first place, stories that no organized mind could ever have comprehended. 'Begin at the beginning and when you come to the end, stop' [Humpty Dumpty's advice to Alice in *Alice in Wonderland*] is just so much nonsense to them, and contrariwise, the rest of Lewis Carroll makes perfectly good sense. As a matter of fact, things like Alice being part of the Red King's dream,[*] and the idea of running as fast as you can to stay in the same place, and the woods where nothing has a name, all these things are very Indian.

Here there are mosquitoes compared with which the Shelter Island proponents are as rare as snow in August and as small as electrons. The mosquitoes here are so big that you first know they are at you when you feel the wind that their wings make. At night you have to jump under the mosquito net, and in a few minutes you can hardly read, because such a thick cloud of mosquitoes has formed on the outside of the net that it almost blocks the light... And

---

[*] I wrote about this in *Dreams, Illusion and Other Realities* (1984), and again in *The Dream Narrative: Dreams of God and Mortals in Classical Hinduism* (2022).

there are real big insects, combining the worst qualities of spiders, cockroaches, and bees, as big as little eggs, that fly into things at night, and make such a racket flopping about that first I thought a dog had gotten into the room. In the morning there is a great heap of dead insects around the light, and you have to sweep it away with a broom. Now that the rains are ending there should be less of them, but still I laugh ha ha at the Shelter Island branch. Like Alice, now I should think nothing of falling off a house.*

Punjab, Chanchal's home, was the early home of the Aryans before they moved down into the Gangetic valley. Punjabis are fierce and volatile, mostly of the warrior castes, and have had violent troubles: being near [what later became] Pakistan,† they were in the thick of Partition violence (remember Chanchal's tales?) and before that they had some 'unpleasantries' with the British (you may have heard of the Amritsar massacre). And before that, the Sikhs terrorized them, carrying off the young girls and that sort of thing. (Chanchal says a Sikh will do something and then think why he has done it: they have their brains in their heels, and so it takes a long time for a thought to come out of the head. She also says that most of Punjab is plains, not mountains.)

---

* In *Alice in Wonderland*, Alice remarks, after falling down the rabbit hole, 'After such a fall as this, I shall think nothing of tumbling down stairs! ... Why, I wouldn't say anything about it, even if I fell off the top of the house!'

† Though, after Partition in 1948, and when Chanchal spoke to me in 1963, the Indian state of Punjab was indeed in India, and 'near Pakistan', Lahore, where Chanchal grew up, before Partition, could not have been near (not yet existent) Pakistan; after Partition it became part of Pakistan.

I haven't forgotten about my heritage; not by a long shot. Being without it makes it all the more vivid to me. As a matter of fact, I was explaining Judaism to Chanchal only yesterday, and was surprised and gratified to find that she knew a great deal about Nazism and was quite violent about it, thinking that she would have preferred to have seen Eichmann tortured a lot before he was killed (Punjabis are very violent) and wishing she could get her hands on Hitler. It didn't surprise me coming from Chanchal, who always feels the right way about everything; though the Indians in general think of World War II as one war like any other, Chanchal feels strongly the implications of attempted genocide: it was she who told me about the British committing the most heinous of sins in trying to create, and almost succeeding, a people Indian in appearance and lineage and English in mind and heart, a most insidious kind of genocide, to save the trouble and expense of importing their office-workers.

17. October 9, 1963,
Shantiniketan

It is getting cool here now, and the days shorter, which feels funny, because the climate is still summer to me even though the sun knows it's autumn. Like the RLS [Robert Louis Stevenson] poem, 'In winter I get up at night and dress by yellow candlelight; in summer it's the other way—I have to go to bed by day', but even more confusing, for in summer I get up at night here, and see the sunrise while the snakes go back into their holes.

I am still moved by the way the Indians treat human

beings at the extremities of life. While we civilized non-Indians were putting infants to work in factories, and even in this century before Freud came into vogue, when we were sending them to bed without supper and making them act like small adults all the time, already—and long before that, too—the Indians knew that children are far more special than mere incipient adults, and have always spent half their time on special things for children—special foods and clothing and stories, special games and the *best* of everything, not 'give the best piece to Daddy and let the children have what fell on the floor, they don't know any better'; and most of all, they love to play with their children, play with them all day long; and, realizing that the children are the ones who know what's up, the adults make themselves like them, instead of trying to bridge the gap the other way. And old people, too, are treated as special human beings, not just worn out, unproductive hangers-on. When grandparents are lonely, their children send the grandchildren to stay with them and keep them company, and since grandparents know wonderful stories and cook delicious candies, it is no chore to visit them. I was talking with Chanchal about this, and I said, 'Of course, you don't really have the problem that we have in the United States, where everyone lives so much longer,' and she answered, 'It comes down to the same thing. Here, old age starts much sooner.' The ingredients of temple worship here are like the ingredients of bread: fire, flowers (flour) and water. I guess it's a kind of Eucharist, forming the blood and body of Shiva (but they don't eat it, not being cannibals like the Christians, or even carnivores, which would prevent them from eating Vishnu even when he was a fish or wild boar*).

I was walking in the sunset with a Bengali girl, and she kept her back to the sun, and I asked her why she didn't look at it, it was so beautiful, and she said she had seen it so many times, and when I told Chanchal what she had said, Chanchal said, 'Why she eats?'

I picked a bunch of golden suli flowers, and my hands were stained for days; I then discovered that the Buddhists have dyed their saffron robes with suli flowers for many centuries.

Chanchal (who, being a Punjabi Hindu and hence no lover of Muslims, is not to be taken on this subject without a grain of salt) told me about the Muslim marriage ceremony.† The groom is asked, 'Will you accept so and so, even if she is deaf and dumb, crippled or diseased?' (None of this richer or poorer for them: poorer is taken for granted, and so is sickness: what remains is what *kind* of sickness.) If he says yes, and the bride agrees, then they are brought together, the bride veiled, and they sit down and are covered by a silk sheet that forms a tent over them, and they bend their heads, and there is a mirror beneath them, and the bride removes her veil, and he first sees her reflected in the mirror. But if the bride doesn't want to marry him, then when they ask her about deaf and dumb, etc., and will she accept him, she says, 'He is like a

---

* Two of Vishnu's animal avatars. He also became a tortoise, a man-lion, and a horse.

† That is, her version of a Muslim marriage ceremony, which deviates in many ways from the actual ceremony.

pig to me.' And that's the end of that, none of your mincing 'If anyone knows why these two should not be joined...', and it is really strong if you think of what Muslims think of pigs.

Here is a very old story that, whatever its cosmological significance, tells a lot about the attitude of fathers towards sons-in-law, and the necessity for saving leftovers in a poor country: Tvastr (the Vulcan or Hephaestus of India, smith of the gods) had a daughter who married the sun, but his brilliance was too much for her to bear, so she fashioned a mortal image of herself, called Shadow, and ran away from the sun. When he found out, much later, about the substitution, he went angrily to Tvastr. (She had gone to her father's house, and he kept on saying and saying, 'You must go back to your husband,' but he let her stay for several thousand years just the same.)

Tvastr explained that the sun was too bright to give pleasure to a woman, and so, with the sun's grateful acquiescence, he mounted the sun on his potter's lathe, and shaved off some of the excess brilliance, making the sun round and handsome. She went back to him (after he found her wandering around as a mare, and, becoming a stallion, mated with her in the mouth: she, suspecting that he was perhaps not her husband, made him discharge the semen through her nose.

I guess this is a kind of elaborate contraception to avoid a child out of wedlock. I like that it says she wasn't *sure* whether or not it was her husband, and so she struggled) and lived happily ever after. And Tvastr used the leftover pieces he had shaved from the sun to make a weapon for

Vishnu. Waste not, want not, or make hay *with* the sun's shine.[*]

Life imprisonment here is for eighteen years. No optimists they.

Even here, people say that the beggars—who look like the people found in Nazi concentration camps, living skeletons—people say that they spend the money you give them on toddy, as people in America say of the down and outs on Broadway.

18. October 10, 1963, *Shantiniketan*

Yesterday I went to visit a tiny village called Amarkutir, which means 'My hut'. On the way we passed a small thatched hut with a sign proclaiming it as a Grand Hotel and it was touching. I couldn't help but think that this was a Grand Hotel in which nothing ever *did* happen.[†] A little farther on we passed a group of houses with a sign saying 'Gandhi Memorial Leper Foundation'. I discovered that it was no longer in use, a short-lived memorial.

It was a day of strange light, dark grey sky but bright sun coming through the clouds, picking out blinding colours in the rice fields and lotus ponds. By the road, under a tree by a pond, there was a merchant asleep, and beside him were two beautiful brass pots connected by a

---

[*] This story about Saranyu or Samjna (whose name I don't even mention in this letter) was one that I wrote about on several occasions, from *Splitting the Difference* (1999) to *Winged Stallions and Wicked Mares* (2021). I got some of the details wrong in this first telling.

[†] In the film *Grand Hotel* (1932), where all sorts of things happen, a permanent resident of the hotel keeps saying, 'People come, people go. Nothing ever happens.'

supple bamboo pole that, when put across the shoulders, bounces high at every dancing step. There was no sound, and no living creature but the grazing cows, and as he slept I half expected a genie to proposition him, or a god to turn his brass pots into gold, or that he would wake up in another country—there was something so story-book about the scene, something suggesting that nothing else in the world existed but that man, and that tree, and that pond, and those two brass pots.

Then came a forest of palm trees, with a path running straight down the middle, and little boys running down the path just as we run through orchards, but here the path was flooded with water, and bright rice stalks grew in it. The trees had cuts along the trunk: they tap the palm trees for toddy and hang buckets from the taps for the liquid to run into, just like tapping maple trees for syrup. Then in the distance I saw a pond, shimmering and vague and deserted, with only miles of flat red clay and green rice fields between me and it, and all around the water grew the white *kash* plants like feathers, as if a flock of swans, or even angels, were drinking at the pond, and they might have been angels, for all I know: the pond seemed to recede as we approached, as if it were a mirage, and we never reached it, but saw it always shining in the distance, framed by the soft *kash*.

19. October 15, 1963, *Shantiniketan*

I sometimes wish that I could forget more about home than I do. Other Americans that I meet tell me that the most unpleasant aspect of dysentery or influenza (you can't have one without the other, as the song goes,* and I had a mild case of both) is the depression that invariably takes hold of you afterwards. I guess that's what made me so homesick. I hit an all-time low when, feeling a little glum, I decided to read some of P.G. Wodehouse's letters to cheer me up. I opened the book (called *Performing Flea*) only to find the first letters, from the 1920s, datelined Great Neck (17 Beverly Road, to be exact). Well, that nearly done me in, but then Chanchal came and told me the delightful story about the crow and the sparrow [see below] and I felt better.

It's hard work, sometimes, being a schizophrenic on mind-heart lines; the scholar in me is having a grand time but sometimes the little girl takes over and no amount of Mysterious East seems worth a fraction of a Late Show or a lunch at the Overseas Press Club, and then I can either force myself to work, which invariably cheers me up, or, if things are bad, I can't work, and just go around telling myself how it is good for me to grow up a little the hard way. But now that I am on top of things again, I guess it's fair game to admit the hard times that have passed.

This morning I was awakened out of a lovely dream of a delicatessen, in which I was ordering pomegranates and prune yogurt to go, when I heard the sound of a loud transistor radio. Transistor radios always sound the same to me, no matter what they are playing, and they conjure up an image of Jones Beach or teenagers turning corners

* 'Love and Marriage' (1955, Sammy Cahn).

on two wheels with the radio at full blast. It took me a few minutes to realize that what I was hearing was the Indian equivalent of Midnight Mass on Xmas, a ceremony at sunrise one week before Durga Puja, in which they pray for the goddess to come to their home. The priest chants in a very exciting way, raising his voice a pitch on every line, until it reaches the very height of his lower register, and then the singing comes in, voices all in their lower registers, though sometimes rising quite high, so that it gives the impression of spontaneous voices, but actually very beautifully modulated. The Bengali girls had all gotten up to hear it, sitting in the lounge with blankets wrapped around them in the dark, with the light of the transistor radio glowing in the centre. It was almost sunrise, so I thought that as long as I was up at such an ungodly (Durga forgive me) hour I might as well see the sunrise. I went up on the roof terrace, wrapped myself in a blanket, and sat listening, though still very sleepy. I could hear the sound of the chants, regular and ancient, but at the same time I began to hear the sounds from the Santhal village, louder and wilder, a strange kind of band music with drums beating out a jazzy military tattoo and at the same time a motley set of instruments playing an Indian tune—a squeaky trumpet, a few Indian flutes, and, of all things, a bagpipe. It was quite an unearthly sound, and I fear that unless Durga is a lover of cacophony she is not going to come and visit.

Last night in the village everyone got drunk, and on the road I met a man shouting the most marvellous song, a combination of Danny Kaye double talk, Satchmo scat, a little boy's imitation of a train, and Vachel Lindsay's

'Congo'. He had a grand time, and so did we who listened to him. That toddy must be grand stuff. It was a beautiful night, dark and soft, with shapes melting in and out of the darkness—a bullock cart, a pond with steps leading down to the water, a woman walking by with a beautiful brass pot on her head, fireflies and shooting stars so close that you could not tell which was which. Walking down the street, everyone sang a song to himself, not wavering a bit from the tune or the rhythm when he passed another singer. Along the road little shops and stalls had candles burning cheerfully, lighting up just a small space, and across the paddy fields you could see the fires blazing in front of the huts. Something small brushed by me, and I looked down to see a tiny boy, naked, wearing just a string under his round belly, covered with dust; he came up to my knees, and was running like a little animal, and he really seemed like a happy little animal, like the little baby that turned into a little pig in *Alice in Wonderland*—this lovely boy might have been going in either direction. The pigs here are just that size, small, furry, and very noisy and lively. And at night everything becomes alike; only the big things exist, says Kalidasa [the most famous Sanskrit poet].

This morning the parades have continued, with floats made of garlands of flowers, and little boys running after them, and an old man carrying a bouncing bamboo cage filled with gorgeous parrots, and beautiful Santhal women, the beautiful arch of their backs showing clearly above the saris that cling to their hips, some of them nursing babies as they walked.

A few nights ago there was a performance of a Yatra, a

medieval Indian play where the whole cast sits on the floor
in the centre of the room (or courtyard, in the old days)
and one or two of them get up and say a few lines, and the
others sing and play instruments. It was a very casual sort
of thing, with a wonderful set of animals—a lion, a jackal,
a frog, all wonderfully designed and impersonated—and the
audience taking part in it in their own way (when one actor
showed 'a picture of his auntie' to another, the children in
the audience cried out, 'Show it to us, too!'), and people
singing even if they couldn't. Singing isn't really the word
for it, for they more often shout the songs, but in tune, as
children shout 'I'm the king of the mountain'. The songs
are lovely, and there is a wonderful point at which they
suddenly change from slow to fast, like the tricky break
in the third chorus of Bix [Beiderbecke]'s 'Since My Best
Gal Turned Me Down'.

More about Chanchal: She is always spilling things on
herself and her surroundings; yesterday I teased her about
it, and she said, 'Every day is Holi with me' (Holi is the
spring festival in which everyone throws coloured powder
on everyone else, like our streamers on New Year's Eve).
She wears the bindi dot on her forehead like the other
women, but hers is always off-centre. Speaking of a servant,
she said, 'You give her a little rope, she gets much looser.'

A few days ago, I went down to the station, and as
I watched the train pull in from Calcutta, people were
hanging on all over it and shouting and jumping around
on the engine, like children with a toy train; they get a
terrific kick out of all mechanical things, and never forget
how silly it all is.

I think the biggest distortion in my understanding of Indian life is the difficulty in getting used to the things that they are used to and considering striking the things that they consider striking. This is the problem of translating words, too; what has the weight of a cliché in one tongue may become striking and charming in translation, throwing off the balance of ideas meant in the original. I don't think this is an easy thing to get over, because it goes right down to your deepest associations. Still, it's fun to try.

Yubon, the girl from Thailand, asked me to correct an essay she had written about Shantiniketan. I came across the sentence, 'I mostly like the pity in the fields.' I knew she was an ardent Buddhist, but I didn't quite know what to make of this, and when I asked her, she said, 'You know, pity, physical training' (called P.T. at Shantiniketan).

India seems to be the land of homesickness, and not just because I see it through homesick eyes. To stay alive, people have to move all the time, separate from their families, learn a new language. Almost everyone I know comes from somewhere else, and when people meet there is always a momentary shuffling of tongues until they decide in which of the many Indian languages of which each has a smattering they might best communicate: one knows Gujarati well and a little Hindi and less Bengali, the other knows Bengali well, a little Hindi and less Gujarati, so they settle on Hindi. Everyone is fiercely proud of his province, his language, his music, and adopts only with a great deal of criticism the culture of the province to which he has been forced to move. They are as proud of the group of huts which flood or famine or Partition caused them to leave behind as the Brits are of their lost ancestral castles.

Chanchal has taught me to play Ludo, her favourite game, which turns out to be none other than Parcheesi [the Indian game of Pachisi].

At night the insects swarm in thick masses around the lights, almost blotting out the light, and in the morning they are all dead on the ground, forming a bed that goes crunch when you walk over it before the sweepers come and clean it out.

Something that one cherishes as especially precious is known as 'a widow's son'.

Yesterday they came and cut away the little tree that grows outside my window, trimming it down to the stem. It grows so fast that in a week it will be back up to the roof, but for now the light comes straight in, and my little friend the yellow bird is finding his solace elsewhere. The clipping of the trees has filled the air with a fine, sweet, minty smell. They are also going to burn down the fields, so that the snakes won't breed in them.

Now that I am on better terms with Bengali, I realize that the presence of English words is an insult to *their* language, not to mine. For Bengalis to have to sound out 'tee-ya-tar' (theatre) or 'chay-ar' (chair) or 'glisherin shope' (glycerine soap) is to have to admit that their own cultural version of these things was rejected by the dominant colonial culture in India, as was their word for them. There is a very bitter Tagore poem that expresses this, called 'The Plump, Crying Tiger'. Here is my translation of it:

> There was a plump, crying tiger, with spots, black, on his body.
> Entering a house to eat a bearer, he saw himself in a mirror.

He went up to the bearer and asked him, 'I want glisherin
shope [*sic*].'
The boy said, 'I've never heard of it in my life. I'm of low
caste.
English, Shminglish [literally: *Ingrij tingrij*], I don't know it.'
The tiger said, 'You must be lying. I have two eyes to see
with.
How could you have gotten the spots off your body without
glisherin shope?'
The boy said, 'I'm black as Krishna. I never rub anything
on me like that.
You make me laugh. I'm no sahib [i.e. white man].'
The tiger said, 'Shame on you. I'm going to eat you.'
The boy said, 'Chi, chi, you would lose face by that.
Don't you know, I'm an untouchable, a disciple of Mahatma
Gandhi.
If you eat my flesh, you will lose caste.'
'My, my, Ram, Ram,' said the tiger,
'It would be a scandal in the tigers' quarters, and
My daughter's marriage hopes would be destroyed.
The tiger goddess would be angry. Never mind the glisherin
shope.'

The satire on English colonialism, while pretty much self-
explanatory, might be clearer if I explain that the words
'glycerine soap' are sound-for-sound transliterated into
Bengali, as so many names of non-Indian things are; also
that the tiger came to eat the boy in the first place, though
he makes it seem that he is just doing it as punishment for
there being no glycerine soap; and 'sahib' is, here, a very
bitter word for a white man, though, as a matter of fact,
it is the only word used for a white man even when no
bitterness is particularly meant.

Then, too, these English words embedded in Bengali are a reminder of the British dominance, and of the sense of inferiority it has given to Indians in ways less obvious than the matter of caste (which they always had, of course, but which the British played upon for their own purposes) and servitude.

It is the realm of material things that particularly undermines their national pride. Indian machine-made things like paper, soap, and plumbing are not as good as foreign machine goods on which there is a very high tariff. So people have gotten into the habit of saying, 'Oh, is this Indian soap? It must be no good,' and so, little by little, some people begin to feel that even their paintings and mountains probably aren't as good as foreign ones. (This is not true of Shantiniketan people, who know how to value their heritage.) Modern India is neither fish nor fowl, and the psychological disturbance amounts to a national identity crisis, expressing itself in such little discordant notes as hearing a Vedic ceremony broadcast over a transistor radio.

Here are two little Punjabi children's stories that Chanchal told me, pure Indian, I think, but of universal appeal:

A crow had a piece of rice, and a sparrow had a piece of grain. They decided to cook them to make pilau, and the crow went for water while the sparrow (a lady) cooked. But she ate the pilau herself, and then deposited some turds in the oven. The crow, returning, seeing what she had done, found her where she was hiding, and then, heating up a pin in the oven, he shoved it up her ass. 'Chi, chi,' said the sparrow, 'don't put that up me like that.' 'Why do you eat other peoples' pilau?' was his only answer. The end.

Next story: A parrot liked to eat grain from the farmers' fields, and his wife warned him, 'Look out, or you'll be caught.' Sure enough, one day he was caught, and she flew up to him, saying, 'I told you so.' 'Wait and see,' he said, 'I'll get free and come back to you.' Hearing this, the farmer cut his head off, but the parrot continued to tell his wife that he would come back to her. Angry, the farmer chopped him up, cooked him, and ate him, but still the parrot said, 'I will come back' (or should I say, 'I shall return,' like MacArthur). Finally, the farmer told two friends to come with him next morning when he 'went to the fields' (i.e. went to the outhouse, but without an outhouse) and wait until the parrot came out and hit him with a sword. Sure enough, the parrot stuck out his head and flew away, and the two friends, swinging at him, killed the farmer. The end.

20. October 20, 1963,
Calcutta

I have been delightfully busy and will continue to be so. I have discovered that Calcutta, like New York, is poor on the outside, but inside you can get anything, for a price. And there are all sorts of different societies and levels, even idle rich who give cocktail parties and spend all their time at the races. This seems a special insult in such a poverty-stricken city, but I suppose in the long run no more so than the idle rich of America.

So much to tell, I hardly know where to begin, but I suppose the beginning is as good a place as any. The night before I left Shantiniketan they held the Ananda Mela ('Joy

Bazaar'), a kind of glorified church bazaar, completely local
and jolly and full of stalls and things to buy made by the
children and garlands and pitching pennies and like that.
Very jolly. That night, Chanchal and I talked late (being
about to part for a month, and maybe more) and she told me
that her father had, in keeping with a technically obsolete
but actually common upper-class Indian tradition, taken a
courtesan some years ago, a woman who was both a Muslim
and a professional prostitute, and had eight children by her
over the years (Chanchal says three of them aren't his, as
any fool can see, any fool but her father, of course), and
now he wants to bring the woman to live with Chanchal's
mother, which is hurting her as much as it would any
woman, Indian or not, to have her husband's mistress under
her roof. To some extent it's another example of the worst
of both worlds—Indian unofficial sanction of the situation,
and a more culturally general sensitivity to it—but even
within its own world it has always been a difficulty; the
most common word for 'enemy' in Sanskrit, used freely for
natural and military enemies as well as social, is the word
which means, primarily, 'co-wife'. I can't make up my mind
whether or not honesty is the best policy here, whether it
is better to make the husband conceal the mistress and let
you hold your head up, or better to come out in the open
with it; it is a sticky situation any way. Chanchal greatly
sympathizes with her mother and wants to go and live
with her in Punjab; this means that she will not consider
marrying a Bengali man whom she might otherwise quite
seriously think of marrying. Love in separation again,
and still again, for in Calcutta (to get ahead of my story)

I found that the son of the family with which I was going to stay is unable to marry the girl he loves, because she is a Brahmin and he a Kshatriya. What makes this more poignant for me is that in all other ways they seem so completely cosmopolitan; the house is full of Perry Mason books and Coca-Cola, but in this most important of all things, of course, one's roots assert themselves; there is an Indian saying: 'Whatever colour the land is, that colour the water is,' and I have found this to be more true of myself, too, than I had ever thought. To add to the list of Indians in separation: the mother of this same Kshatriya boy, a lovely, strong woman who runs a school for two-year-old children (that's starting early, by God), is not living with her husband, and seems quite lonely.

Well, the next morning I left for Calcutta, a crazy train ride (at the station they were slaughtering chickens for the railway restaurant, and little boys kept stooping to kiss my feet; the third-class carriage was so full I had to get in through the window) but a most beautiful one. The scenery from the train had that magical light upon it, misty and supersharp. In the distance, all was purple and infinitely far away; nearer, the glorious paddy fields stretching for miles like another green sky beneath the dimmer blue one, and in the foreground single figures with a compelling, mythological simplicity. Here, a thatched hut, or a tent of coconut leaves, is like a tree or an animal's home; they do not challenge nature with strange materials and awkward shapes, and so their sweet, vague houses blend in with the land, making the deserted places alive and the inhabited places peaceful. A palm tree rose curved out of a sea of paddy, alone, asserting itself, sticking out its chest; a heron was mirrored in a pool, looking very aesthetic, or flew low over the fields, casting a dazzlingly sharp shadow, looking very holy, as if he had just flown out of the heart of some dying saint, or just perched on the head of a bullock submerged in the paddy fields, looking very funny. The whole scene captured the essence of mythology; each figure was the only thing that existed, and each was not merely itself but all the things it stood for. Even the ugly things became beautiful as they flickered between art and life; the intricate twisting of the trunk and roots of an ancient banyan tree, like an aged, aged man,* a pile of bricks where someone had foolishly tried to build a house that would last longer than the others—even the naked bodies of the crippled and diseased, being so honestly exposed, took on a Biblical simplicity and peacefulness. The climate here calls all the shots, and there is something satisfying, as well as terrifying, in that—the rain and the sun being *everything*, you have to pray to them, and if you still fail, well, you just pray harder next year. At least it removes the terrible elements of ambition and self-criticism which so plague America.

(*Continued in Part IV*)

---

* The title of a poem by Lewis Carroll, embedded within *Through the Looking Glass*.

Part Four

CALCUTTA

Reading, in this section, the stupid, vapid, highfalutin' philosophical posturings and biased political generalizations of my younger self, representing as the opinions of all Indians the views of a few hotheaded Bengalis and Punjabis—particularly their virulent hatred of Nehru, which I did not share—in passages that were really not central to my own intellectual agendas and that now make me wince, I was tempted to cut them all out. Even while I was in India, I began to suspect (as in the letter of November 24, 1963) that it was just some of my crazy friends, and not all Indians, who hated Nehru. (It is also not clear to me even now how I processed Chanchal's deeply skewed bias against Muslims.) But then I thought, well, those passages do provide an occasion to think about the infantile beginnings of a serious scholar. And so I kept them in.

∽

20. October 20, 1963 (Continued)

Well, such were my thoughts as I rode to Calcutta, but, as always, the practical invaded the domain of the aesthetic, and I found myself hoping in spite of myself that the people I was going to stay with (a family from Shantiniketan) would have hot water to wash with, and a fan. My every hope was surpassed; everyone fell over backwards to please me; fresh fruit and fans, to say nothing of air-conditioners, were at my disposal, and when I arrived, tired and hot, I was given time to shower and then, when I met the mother, who was about to take a nap on an enormous bed full of cushions and pillows and blankets, in an air-conditioned room, she said, 'You must be tired; come, lie down beside me and take a nap,' and I did, and how cool and safe and even at home I felt. Then I woke up and had a bite to eat (including milk from the cow tethered out in the back yard, visible from my bedroom window on the third floor).

Then Seeta (the Brahmin girl) took me to visit her hospital, for she is a medical student. I walked into a room with a table on which someone was being held down while his foot was cut open; in another room there were nine naked women in labour, and in another I was handed a minutes-old, wet, new-born baby 'to kiss, because it's so cute', and before I knew what was happening, there it was in my hands, so I handed it back. I went into a room where there were foetuses in bottles, labelled with the woman's name; the first one I saw was named Shakuntala [the name of the heroine of Kalidasa's famous Sanskrit play]. There are a hundred babies born every night in the maternity ward, and it is called (named after some British donor, no doubt, but still strikingly appropriate for a maternity ward) Eden. Everywhere in the hospital there were cats wandering around and people lying everywhere, on the roofs, in the halls, on the staircases, everywhere. One man was dying slowly of a liver disease, and Seeta told me proudly that she had kept him alive for a month longer than anyone had thought he could live. I asked why she tried, since there were people who needed the bed and might live much longer. 'I do it because he specially asked me to,' she said. 'He wants very much to live.' The venereal disease clinic is open only at night, because people are ashamed to come during the day.

As we rode home on the bus, I realized that I was beginning to know Calcutta, to recognize landmarks, to hear the sounds of the language, to read the signs, and I was not at all frightened, as I had been when I first came to India. But much of my friendliness towards Calcutta is due to the Dimocks. The day after my visit to the hospital with Seeta, I went to call on the Dimocks, as they had requested me to call on them when I came to Calcutta. When I arrived, they were at breakfast, and they asked me to join them, and they said that they had a guest room all ready for me and had been expecting me to stay with them. And from that moment on, I was cured of all diseases mental, emotional, and physical. Physically, they took me to the best doctor in Calcutta (they had been going to him themselves because one or two of the children were always sick with something or other) and gave me a couple of square meals and what with that and all the more subtle comforts, I am completely well now and feeling like I'm glad I'm me. Mentally, it's been a regular resuscitation: Ed Dimock has been working with me on the Bengali mythological texts, making me glad I've done so much Bengali at Shantiniketan, and we've been talking about India and mythology and literature and translation.

With perfect timing, just as we were discussing the Dudley Fitts contribution to translation technique,* a letter arrived for me forwarded from Shantiniketan by Chanchal right after we left, and it was a letter from Fitts himself, answering, in the most delightful spirits, a letter I had written to him about a book he had asked me about. The letter began: 'What a tremendous *strophe* your address makes, what *cola*, what *membra*, what *periodi*! One finds oneself (hell, I'm talking about myself)—I find myself declaiming it in the bath: Bírla Hòstel/Vídya Bhavän, VīSva Bhāráti, Sántiníketan/Bólpúr (Bolp Up?)/Birbhum (so named for the inferiority of its ale)/&c. It demands an antistrophe, but only the ear of a Maus could supply it.' And on like that, but even better, because his typewriter can do all sorts of tricks. It really made me feel good to get it, and to get it just then, making me feel like a Scholar Among Scholars.

And to add to the list of mental comforts, Ed Dimock knows all the great people in Calcutta, and is taking me to see them all this next week, Sanskritists and Bengali scholars, and is determined to make me like Calcutta enough that I will stay here instead of going on to Benares after my Delhi trip, and at this rate he seems likely to succeed. But most of all, it has been such a tremendous emotional booster for me to find the Dimocks such grand friends. Mrs Dimock and I had a terrific talk about the kind of reaction that sets in when you get so angry at the Bengalis for wanting to make you a Bengali that you don't

---

* Fitts was a famous translator, with whom I had taken a workshop at Harvard.

even want to give them the satisfaction of teaching you the Bengali things you *do* want to know. This is tricky to explain, but I went through it a while back and had been feeling guilty about it, and it's so good to find it par for the course. Similarly, we agreed that nothing makes you feel so American as being away from America for a while, and the only way you can understand India is through your own prejudices. This is what I meant when I was thinking about the translating of clichés, about how hard it is to be struck only by what strikes them, but now I realize it's not hard, it's impossible, and, more than that, it is not a desirable thing at all. This in literature as well as in life: the thing that charms is the idea of a woman being beautiful if she walks like a female elephant; to translate this as 'she walks as gracefully as a cat' is to miss the whole point, and it is equally pointless [for an American] to try to feel that it isn't *funny* to think of a female elephant's walk as graceful. The value this metaphor has for a non-Indian reader is humour, which must be accepted as replacing the beauty which it really holds for an Indian reader. And with living here, too, you can only like what *you* like; I like animals and children and mountains and good stories, and I *don't* like spicy food or a tropical climate or Making Friends For America, and all the Gandharvas in the heavens telling me I should doesn't make a bit of difference. I can't tell you how relieved I feel to be supported in this sort of view. Having been surrounded by people whose feelings and views were so foreign from mine, I lost a sense of the value of my own feelings, and really the only time when I felt sure at all of my views was when I wrote these letters. But now, living with the Dimocks, I can be an American in India; and my kind of American, too, liked for myself, not for my friendly efforts to absorb India.

I went out and bought little toys for all the children (there are five, all under ten years old, and they get restless indoors, as they can't play on the street), and the oldest girl combs my hair and braids it, and they let me read their Dr Seuss books to them, and they show me their grasshoppers, and I correct their subtraction homework, and the Dimocks have a terrific jeep, and we all pile in, all eight of us, and the driver, and go to the market or to see the animal market where there are monkeys and things, and at night we sit on the terrace drinking rum and water and telling jokes and stories and really have a grand time, and Mr Dimock (he has asked me to call him Ed, but I can't bring myself to do it yet) plays the guitar, and we all sing. I sewed a hem for one of the little girls, and we are going to a friend's house to see the Puja celebration at home, and yesterday we took a jeep ride to the south of the city where we saw a very strange temple: it's a temple to which both Muslims and Hindus go before they enter the jungle, to pray that they won't be eaten by tigers, and the statue is not, as we had thought, a statue of a tiger but a white sahib with a gun! And at night I have a lovely room with a fan, and an icebox to raid. My cup runneth over.

21. October 28, 1963,
c/o Dimock, 12/2 Swinhoe Street,
Calcutta – 19

I am very busy here and learning much, though not much from books. The book learning will start in a month, when

I come back to Calcutta from Shantiniketan and Delhi. The Dimocks have invited me to come and live with them when I get back from Delhi, and I may do it; it certainly would be great fun, and my only hesitation would come from the fact that I would be monopolizing one of the guest rooms meant to accommodate Institute scholars passing through Calcutta. Still, no matter where I stay in Calcutta (and it looks like I will stay in Calcutta, just taking a few weeks off to go and see Benares, but not to study there), I will be spending most of my time here.

The Dimocks took me to see Jamini Roy, one of India's finest painters, and I bought a beautiful painting which is being sent to you Air Mail. Unroll it when it gets there, and see how you like it; if you're crazy about it, I might see my way to parting with it, but otherwise I'll keep it for myself, because I love it. If you really like it, I can get more from him; this one cost about $30.

I've started making a list of things I'd like you to bring when you come in January: a bottle of Midol pills, a half dozen rolls of Kodachrome film, and as much Scotch and Vermouth as you can get in Free Port on the way over. (Ed Dimock, like the good Unitarian Minister that he is, likes to have a couple at night, and he desperately misses martinis; I owe them much, and would like to give him some liquor as a present. Gin is easy to get here,* but Vermouth is fabulously expensive.)

Life at the Dimocks' house is like living *Cheaper by the*

---

* I later discovered that most of the gin was manufactured by moonlighters under Howrah Bridge, until so many people went blind from drinking it that the police destroyed all the stills.

Dozen.* When I first came here looking for the house (the numbers in Calcutta are entirely random, with 12 between 47 and 78), the people I asked said, 'You mean a thin man with lots of children?' and that's what Ed Dimock is. At their house in Chicago they have fourteen cats, and the house here has the same feeling. The kids stand on the roof and call out to the balloon sellers and banana sellers and monkey sellers on the street, and they all come up and usually they manage to sell something before they leave. Politicians and artists and newspapermen and scholars troop in and out speaking various languages and tripping over the books and pits and birds that litter the floor; everyone stays very late, discussing India and poetry, and Ed Dimock sits there with a glass of rum, looking over the rims of his glasses and laughing at everything. Then we all pile into the car and go somewhere, which is always an adventure; the streets are full of goats and cows and rickshaws and people cooking and general mobs that part as the car nudges them and close in again right behind it. It's impossible to drive, so you have to hire a driver; it would be terrible if an American were to run someone down, which is almost inevitable, and if the driver happens to hit someone, the mob comes and beats him up; Ed Dimock has seen several people beaten to death for hitting a pedestrian, as they also occasionally beat a thief to death. The driver we have manages to just miss everyone, and the crazy careenings are made even spicier by the fact that every time he passes a Shiva temple (and there is one on

---

* A 1950 film about a very large and chaotic family.

just about every block) he lifts both hands off the wheel in a reverential gesture, bowing his head at the same time. This only takes a second or two, but the car passes about 500 people in that time, and we all hold our breath.

We took one trip out into the countryside, and in doing so passed through the Calcutta suburbs, which consist of miles and miles of shacks along the road, finally melting into jungle. The jungle itself looked just like Jamaica, or what I have seen of pictures of Hawaii, and it smelled and felt just the same. The sun and the rain are so all-encompassing here that they completely override the human element, the cultural element, and all you can sense is the jungle, like any other jungle. The night there is particularly beautiful, but partly, I think, because the cool Indian night is so welcome after the Indian day. I have been wearing red shoes, and the perspiration made the dye come off on my feet, staining them red just exactly the way that the Indian women paint their feet red. It really seemed like an episode out of *A Passage to India*, where the force of the country claims you in spite of your efforts to resist, wearing you down by small coincidences, absorbing your small self in its greatness.

Many of the Dimocks' friends are mixed couples, an American girl married to a Bengali, a Spanish girl, Conchita, married to another Bengali, and at Shantiniketan I had met an American woman who had lived there for thirty-five years, married to a Bengali. They have a pretty tricky time of it, but they are unusually spirited people, real fighters, and seem to be glad of all of it. There is a loneliness about the women, though; Conchita, who is very soulful, said that not a day goes by when she does not think of Spain, and her husband had been away from India for so long when he married her that the picture he gave her of what their life would be turned out to be quite different from what it really is, with Conchita taking care of a mother-in-law who bathes in Ganges water every time Conchita touches her. The woman at Shantiniketan reminded me of Eleanor Roosevelt, but she had a way of constantly saying 'My husband' in an almost aggressive way that seemed to be a constant reminder to herself as well as to us that he was well worth all the troubles of their life; he is a poet, and she has translated much of his work into English, and they have a pretty busy life, and are completely tied up in each other, partly, I suppose, because there are few Indians with whom they can be close.

Alan Ginsberg was in Calcutta, sleeping under Howrah Bridge, and some of his poems have been translated into literal Bengali, which makes the strangest reading. This kind of 'living with the Indians', which has pretty much gone out of style, is the kind of thing that led Galbraith to walk barefoot in the paddy fields, thus contracting a good case of hepatitis. The Indians still go for it, and are very pleased when you drink out of a soiled cup or a village well, but most Americans, even ambassadors official or unofficial, now take the line that you have to remain American to have an honest international contact, and one of the things that makes you functionally as well as culturally different from an Indian is the habit of clean food, which your body as well as your respect for your own culture insists be maintained in India. Still, to avoid insulting people you have to take what they give you. A couple of nights ago they gave us *bhang lassi*, which is a kind of consciousness-expanding liquid drug; I had only a little, but Ed, being the guest of honour, had to drink all of his, and had some pretty terrifying hallucinations. Still, he did much for the American Image, which is pretty low in some quarters; you hear stories about things like the American couple who hired a taxi for a day, ran up a bill that would feed the driver's family for several weeks (and out of which he had to pay a large fee to the company from which he rented the cab) and then disappeared into a building and never came back to pay. It's hard to tell whether this sort of thing has a greater or smaller effect on public feeling than the larger issues of foreign aid and civil rights in America (which are given wide publicity here).

This has been Durga Puja week, celebrating the time when Durga, the wife of Shiva, returns to her mother's house for four days after she has been married, and then goes away again with Shiva. A week before Durga Puja she is summoned to Calcutta by the sunrise ceremony of chants and songs that I heard at Shantiniketan, and then she comes a week later. All over the city, in crèches made of banners, there are images of Durga, with ten arms, slaying the buffalo demon who represents the miseries of the world. The story goes that after she slew him, she was so impassioned that she went on destroying everything, finally even stepping upon Shiva and opening her mouth to swallow him up too. But then she realized what she was doing and became pacified. She is usually depicted stepping on Shiva with her tongue out; since sticking out the tongue is indicative of surprise in Bengal, one Bengali I spoke to said that she sticks out her tongue because she suddenly realizes, 'Argh! I'm stepping on my husband!' Others maintain that all women walk all over their husbands, and she is merely sticking out her tongue to taunt him. This story is the complement to the one in which Shiva is about to destroy the world, and his wife pacifies him; it comes to the same thing in Hindu cosmology, where the male and female principles must be united to keep the world in balance, and to create.*

The images of Durga are worshipped by beating steel drums in front of them constantly for four days, and it really begins to drive you out of your mind after a while. Yesterday, early in the morning, a goat was sacrificed to Durga, and I got up and walked through the still dark streets to the place where a family was sacrificing its own goat. As the drums began to get louder, the people who were sleeping all over the street began to wake up and walk towards the shrine; the noise became deafening as the boys began to blow on the conch shells and strike metal pots together. The priest sprinkled Ganges water on the goat and talked to him, telling him, as in the *Rig Veda*, 'Don't be afraid, goat. You are going the good going,'† but the little goat wasn't having any. Bleating, he was carried to the sacrificial block, and a string was tied around his head. The priest pulled on his head, and two men pulled on his feet, stretching him out taut. The sword was offered to

* I wrote about Durga and her tongue in *Women, Androgynes, and Other Mythical Beasts* (1980).

† I wrote about the goat in *The Rig Veda: An Anthology* (1981).

Durga to be blessed, and then with one stroke the head was severed from the body, and as it sprang free the priest held it high in the air and carried the head to Durga as an offering. Then the drums stopped, and after reciting a few prayers, the people went away, and I decided I wanted a breath of fresh air.

Later I went to the great temple at Kalighat, and there was a tremendous crowd of people bringing baskets of offerings on their heads, filing past the great image and leaving the offerings. Within the temple there were hundreds of goats waiting to be killed, and there was a great pile of heads in one corner, while in another the dogs were eating the skin and offal. All the beggars in India seemed to be there, and shops selling sweets and garlands and images of the goddess, and people shouting as they poured into the temple, and the bleating of the goats and the chanting of hymns. It was deeply disturbing in a way that the simple sacrifice at dawn had not been. There was a violence and misery about it that I had never imagined before. And right after that I went to the Indian Museum to see the fabulous gem-encrusted statues of the medieval gods, and the serene dancing Shivas, and the contrast was overwhelming. The art in the museum was produced by people worshipping a different kind of a god, perhaps in a different part of the land, in a place of peace and beauty, where a gentle life inspired the worship of a gentle god*— but even then there were terrible, terrible stories of the cruelty of the gods that make Job seem blessed, and these

---

* This stunningly naïve formulation is only partially vindicated by the second half of the sentence, after the dash.

stories were told of the same majestic, serene Shiva that I have always loved. I can't sort it out in my mind; I know that it all goes together, but emotionally it seems impossible to reconcile.

Then the images were all dismantled after the fourth day and taken down and thrown into the Ganges. Everyone was drunk, and as each image came by (there are about five thousand of them, each tremendous and intricately carved and decorated, covered with real garlands and necklaces, each goddess standing on a life-sized, fuzzy lion and killing a half-demon half-buffalo) on bamboo poles on the shoulders of some twenty-five men, it was preceded by a band, the most wonderful music I've ever heard, consisting of flutes, steel drums, skin drums, pipes, bagpipes, brass pots, and conch shells. The rhythm is a combination of the Indian tunes, with their five- or seven-beat syncopation, and the steady beat of a kind of jungle rhythm, and a real jazzy off-beat, and a calypso lilt, and the tune is equally lively and mixed up. All the children carry candles and dance around, really dance, and shout and it's altogether the most fun imaginable. Then, at midnight, we went down to the Ganges and sat by one of the ghats; the river was lit by candles and lights all up and down the bank, and there were thousands of little pole-driven boats floating up and down, lit with candles and overflowing with people. One after another they heaved the great images into the river and dived in after them, shouting and pushing them under the water, then splashing the holy water on everyone, and making way for the next image, and all the time the drums and flutes were playing, and people singing.

22. November 1, 1963,
c/o Dimock

Tonight I leave for Delhi, travelling one day and two nights, first class, on express trains. I love train rides, and look forward to this one, as I have not yet travelled at all in India.* So here are the last of the Calcutta notes.

First of all, when I return from Delhi, I am definitely going to set up shop here in Calcutta. I went to see Professor Hazra to ask him to recommend a teacher for me, and lo and behold he said he would be delighted to work with me himself (*Man geht nicht zum Schmidl*), and his ideas of teaching mesh perfectly with my ideas of learning: instead of going over every word, as the pandits do, and as I feared he would (as he is a deeply religious man, and can somehow regard the Puranas as the autobiographies of the gods, and at the same time discuss the Iranian influences and Dravidian interpolations), he makes the best of both worlds, reading with the enthusiasm of a believer and the acumen of a disbeliever. He will let me work through by myself and send him lists of the difficult spots, and then we will just go over those spots; this way I will be able to get a great deal covered in just a few of his hours every week, and have plenty to keep me busy in between. Besides, I will be working on the Bengali *mangals* and myths, and this is the only place for that; it is also the most intellectually exciting place in India, I think, and the Dimock house is a veritable vortex. The Dimocks really want me to come and stay; I

---

* This was not strictly true, as I had often travelled locally between Calcutta and Bolpur, but clearly I meant travel on express trains across India, which I had not yet begun to do.

have become one of the family, the kids love me, and we sit up into the wee small hours laughing and confiding in each other. So I am well settled. Today we went on a picnic to the zoo as a farewell party for me, and I really feel that I'm leaving home, and will be eager to return.

Several things together have made it possible for me to be at home here. I have finally realized that it is not necessary to love everything about India in order to love India, any more than it is at home, or in a person (being a hero-worshipper and idealizer by nature this is not as obvious for me as it may seem, and I think I will probably have to re-win this same battle many times again, but I have won this round at least). 'The lotus flower grows in mud' is the Indian expression, and the glory of Indian religion grows in blood and poverty. I have learned to see the lotus through the mud, so to speak, and this is the worthwhile aspect of what I spoke of as impossible before, seeing as striking only what is striking to an Indian. It will always be impossible for me *not* to react to the things that are striking to me but not to them—I cannot help reacting to a naked man, or a woman nursing a child, or a tropical sunset, or a dancer in ecstasy. But in a positive way, I am learning to react, in addition, to the things which are significant to them, and which were at first obscured to me by the 'insignificant' facts of Indian life.

Yesterday by Kalighat I saw a woman sitting, squatting, by a bed on the sidewalk, her home; she was carefully taking the lice out of her young daughter's hair. Unlike the Indians, I reacted sharply, for the thousandth time, to the fact that she lived in the street, and that there were

lice, which gives me the shivers. But at the same time I
felt the tenderness of it, the way Indians are about their
children, and I thought of the old Sanskrit verse, 'When
little children ask to sit upon your lap, you are blessed by
the dirt on their bodies.' Now I see the indulgence of the
street children as part of a sadder thing; those parents know
that only in childhood will they have any chance at all to
be happy, to be free from the terrible pain of Indian life,
and so they give them all they have for just those few years.

I was talking to a Bengali man who has six brothers;
they are all wealthy, but none of them intend to marry. I
was teasing him about it and was suddenly moved when
I realized the seriousness of his reasons for not marrying;
he said he was afraid that there would be a famine, or
that the government would keep back the food even if
the crops were good (more about this later), and that he
didn't want to live like a dog the way the others did. And
this is a man who owns a big house and has never had to
work for a day of his life. He just doesn't trust life enough
to involve anyone else in it; he lives with his parents, goes
to the courtesans in Calcutta, and remains 'detached' in a
way that the Indian ascetics never intended. There was
such fear and disgust in his voice as he said that he didn't
want to live like a dog; in America, you would expect some
childhood insecurity or poverty at the root of it, which
he had never known, but just living in Calcutta day after
day would have the same effect on a child as a personal
experience of poverty. I felt myself such a small thing
against the tremendous fact of their poverty, so ridiculous
that I should have so much to their nothing, that I really

felt it needed a constant and tremendous exertion of power to keep such an unnatural situation, such an imbalance, from toppling onto me. And so this man feels his wealth is unsafe, feels it constantly.

This widespread insecurity is also in some obscure way at the heart of the tremendous hatred of Nehru and the government that is growing stronger every day in India, and will, I think, very soon result in his overthrow. I don't know whether it is true or not, but some of the people I have spoken to believe that Nehru is robbing the country. The crops have been good, but still there are shortages, rationing, and widespread black-market operations on rice, sugar, fish, and jute. Prices have rocketed, and the starvation statistics with them. I remember Chanchal telling me how people in Punjab hated Nehru because the man he had put in power there was an out-and-out thief, retaining his power only because he gave Nehru a cut. I thought little of it at the time, but now the Punjabis have had enough and have demanded that the man be removed, and Nehru is refusing to remove him. There is a similar situation in Bengal, which has a government that makes Tammany Hall* look like a charity organization. If Nehru loses Punjab and Bengal there will be terrible trouble, and the way things are going, anything could happen. They hate him, they jeer him, the newspapers attack him, and people feel that the austerities imposed in the name of the 'National Emergency' is just another excuse for graft. There is a common poster in public places, about smallpox, with a picture of Nehru

* The corrupt political machine that ruled New York City from 1789 to 1967.

CALCUTTA   153

and his statement, 'It would be a wonderful thing for us to
wipe out this scourge from India.' The Indians cross out the
reference to smallpox so that the statement seems to refer
to the picture of Nehru. And I can see how Nehru must be
so terrified as to impose his will as he is doing now; living
in Calcutta, the meaning of mobs and riots is something
terrific. But the sad thing is that they have no one to take
his place; even the most rabid of his opponents admit this,
and as long as he is clever enough not to go too far—if he
hasn't already gone too far—no one really knows what to
do about him. 'After Nehru—Who?'* is a title full of more
bitterness than I realized before. He's really batting on a
sticky wicket, and I, selfish to the last, am only glad that
he has been cool to the United States lately. The feeling of
the people I know here is very strongly pro-American, so I
feel the mobs as sympathizers rather than threats, in spite
of such incidents as the shipment of sugar to America and
a leftist movement that criticizes America for purposely
spurring on the Cold War in order to force the weaker
nations of Asia and Africa to join an alliance and form a
market advantageous to American economy.

Well, so much for politicking, and back to random
notes.

There has been a most spirited controversy in the
newspapers here as to whether tigers have a sense of smell
or whether they have a kind of jackal go ahead of them, like
a pilot fish. People are really getting worked up about this.

We went to dinner in an Indian house, and after sitting

---

* The title of a book by Welles Hangen, published in 1963. He was killed
in Cambodia in 1970.

cross-legged and eating all manner of strange things, I discovered, on stiffly rising, that I had been sitting under a photograph of Stalin all the time. The man said, in answer to my question, that not everyone in the house liked Stalin, that each had his own views. One liked Stalin, one Lenin, one Khrushchev, one Bulganin...

The Puja drums have finally stopped, and I must say it is a great relief. I am beginning to understand why the sages take vows of silence, but the *real* cool ones meditate in the midst of all that hellish noise, partly from a concept of 'renouncing renunciation' (which always reminds of the man—was it Mark Twain?[*]—who could resist everything but temptation) and partly, like Gandhi sleeping with his niece, to prove that they can remain firm in the midst of chaos.

The Dimocks know some people who had a piano carried from Bombay to Poona on the heads of eight coolies. It reminded me of the man that got his cat to carry his piano up four flights of stairs—by using a whip.

A woman nearby just died at the age of a hundred and five after having been widowed at the age of five, as often used to happen in India. To be a widow in India for a hundred years is the most terrible life I can imagine, the most perverse fate I have ever heard of.

Five people were arrested last week for doing the twist in front of a statue of the goddess Durga.

The Lone Ranger appears in Bengali newspapers, and instead of 'Hiyo Silver!' he says, '*Thik aache*,' which is an

---

[*] No, it was Oscar Wilde.

all-purpose Bengali expression meaning 'Okay', 'You don't say', 'You're welcome', 'Never mind', 'That's right', and a lot of similar things, none of them 'Hiyo Silver!'

I bought a painting from Jamini Roy, and then I bought a book about Indian painting, mostly ancient but with just one or two modern reproductions, and one of them was my very own Jamini Roy painting!

There is a traditional list of the 'Five M's', five things prohibited to monks*: *matsya, mansa, madya, mudra,* and *maithuna,* which mean 'meat, fish, wine, grain, and sexual intercourse'. I want to translate them as the 'Five F's': I've got flesh, fish, fermented (grapes), farina—but what's a word for sexual intercourse beginning with F?

Yesterday we went to visit a man who has about eight thousand books in his living room. He mentioned that he knew them all by heart; just to kid him, Ed took out a volume, opened to a page, told him the page number and the first word, and I'll be goddamned if the man didn't recite the whole page letter perfect. He knows not only all of Sanskrit literature (I quizzed him on Kalidasa, and was rewarded with a complete recital of *Shakuntala,* for forty-five minutes) and Bengali literature, but *all* of Shakespeare, too.

All day long I drink mango squash, which is sold just like orange squash and lemon squash in the States, but is infinitely more delicious.

My favourite Calcutta signs: 'Anti-rowdy squad' and 'Psycho clinic for problem children'.

---

* Not really; they are the five things generally used in the antinomian Tantric rituals.

I came across a picture of a man having intercourse with a woman who is doing a backbend, and meanwhile he is blowing a trumpet. It's on a temple frieze, and I'd love to see it. I'd like to have it on my coat of arms or something.

Last night I went to see the movie *Sabrina*, with Humphrey Bogart and Audrey Hepburn. I don't know what perversity moved me to it, but, although I had seen it years ago, I completely forgot that the whole cotton-picking mother-loving movie was shot in Glen Cove and Great Neck. For two hours I watched them sailing around the Merchant Marine Academy and driving to New York on the Belt Parkway past LaGuardia, and walking along Northern Boulevard out past Manhasset, where it has the white fences, driving [Mercedes Benz] 190 SLs, and talking about playing polo in Old Westbury. At first it really tore me up, but now that I am healthy again (I keep wondering what you think when I mention that I'm no longer sick, because I think I tried not to tell you that I ever was sick. Oh what a tangled web we weave when first we practise to deceive.* Well, I was sick, but now I'm not, and when I was I didn't know what to do about my homesickness, but now I can handle it) I came out of it feeling how lucky I was to know that life so well, and love it, and still know and love this one, too. There were some scenes of Paris in it, too, and I know a little of Paris, and I know New York, and now Calcutta, and I see things that remind me of Mexico City, and I can't describe it, but it was a very nice cosmopolitan feeling that worked exactly against the

---

* This was one of my mother's favourite lines, from Sir Walter Scott's 1808 epic poem, *Marmion: A Tale of Flodden Field*.

homesickness so that I actually came out of the movie feeling better than before, almost as if I had gotten rid of a big lump of homesickness, just *because* the movie was so very, very close to home.

I was talking to Conchita, and she said that when she first went to London from Spain she wanted to go home, and the only thing that stopped her was her fear that her father would say, 'So. You wanted to see the world.' And she said she would be terribly friendly with Spaniards that she wouldn't even have bothered to spit on in Madrid. And I could really sympathize, but now it isn't that way at all, and it makes me feel good to think of home, because I am beginning to feel Calcutta more and more a kind of home. Last night we even dressed up and took the children Trick-or-Treating to our friends and carved a pumpkin and everything. Of course, we, as Americans, could only go to understanding Americans, but there were enough of them to fill many a paper bag.

I heard the Indian version of our joke about the camel that is made to drink extra water when the man sneaks up behind him and smashes his balls together. In this version, after he does this, a man asks him, 'But doesn't it hurt?' and he answers, 'Only if you get your thumbs caught.'

Part Five

TRAVELS IN INDIA

My knowledge of Indian history here is a bit muddled, to put it mildly. Many peoples came to India before the British, starting with the Indo-Aryans, and then notably the Greeks, Huns, Persians, Turks and Mongols (later called Moguls and still later Mughals). They came as pastoralists, migrants, traders, storytellers, proselytizers, and, finally, conquerors. Sometime in the medieval period, many Indians began to call all the Islamic traders, invaders, and settlers 'Turks', and I apparently called them all 'Arabs'. But I seemed to use 'Mogul' (which I've here corrected to 'Mughal' throughout), and occasionally 'Arab', rather loosely to designate any Turkic or Arabic or Islamic people or culture in India. On top of all this misguided history, the paragraph about the 'Ancient Fort' (Purana Qila; November 22, 1963) is a good example of my rampant Antiquarianism/Orientalism. Moreover, my remarks about Delhi apply only to the modern part of Delhi; I seem not to have explored the larger city, to which I refer once but to which very few of my comments about Delhi are even remotely relevant.

At the same time, in these letters I am still troubled by, and confused about, the beggars, and now (November 22, 1963) I seem to have forgotten what I had written about dealing with beggars in Shantiniketan.

It is a bit tricky to piece together my itinerary from these two long letters. The first letter, dated November

8, 1963, covers my travels first with Mishtuni Roy—to
Delhi and then on to Agra, Mathura, and Vrindavan—
and then, apparently without Mishtuni, to Udaipur,
Khajuraho, Mount Abu, and Chittorgarh. But attached
to this letter is a set of pages that I have labelled '23
A. Miscellaneous travel notes'. These pages, which are
undated, discuss sites in South India and at Elephanta
and Bhubaneshwar that I may have visited alone at
an earlier date or later, with my mother, in January
1964 (see the Postscript). The second and final letter
in this section, dated November 22, 1963, returns to
the description of my travels in North India and, now,
Rajasthan, where the recurrence of the words 'we'
and 'us' seems to imply that I am again travelling with
Mishtuni Roy.

But let us begin with November 8, 1963, in New
Delhi. In a temporary doubling back to the world of
Shantiniketan, I encountered in Delhi rather than back
in Bengal one of the Tagore crowd, Jyotirindra Moitra.
He was born in 1911 (and died in 1977), so he was only
fifty-two when I met him but, like Hazra, he apparently
struck me as old. Popularly known as Botukda, he was
a rather famous composer and lyricist, for film as well
as the stage.

∾

23. *November 8, 1963,*
New Delhi (c/o Kshitish Roy, 21 Rajghat Colony, New Delhi – 1)

We Calcutta people find Delhi antiseptic, like most modern
capital cities. They think themselves very advanced because
they have urinals in the streets, like the Paris ones, but

that only takes care of the urine, and everyone still has
to shit in the street. Transportation is either by horse-
drawn tonga (which I love, but which the Indians hardly
ever let me take, as it is considered primitive) or by a kind
of motorcycle hitched to a two- or four-seated little cart,
very much like the things you bump each other with at a
carnival, and giving the most thank-you-Ma'am*-ridden
ride you can imagine. I'm sure it's knocked several inches
off my ass riding in them, but there must be an easier way.

When I first arrived in Delhi, at the Mukherjee
house [friends of Mishtuni Roy and her father], the old
grandfather was at the window, and told me to come up;
when everyone was making a fuss over me, he kept saying,
'I saw her first,' and I really felt fêted. I was exhausted after
two days on the train, and they insisted that I take a nap in
the big bed; I later found out that it was the grandfather's
bed, and he insisted on letting me sleep in it that night,
while he slept on the floor with the others. There was
absolutely nothing I could do to stop this; he went and lay
down and that was the end of it. But now I am at Mishtuni's
father's house, where I am just one of the family, sharing
a bed with two others, and I feel more at ease. Mishtuni's
father, Kshitish Roy, is a famous poet and knows the most
wonderful people, but as they are quite poor and refuse to
let me help to pay for food, etc., I feel uneasy about staying
here too long.

A few nights ago, we went to see the Ramlila, the

---

* This is a phrase, current in our family, for a bump in the road that makes
your vehicle leave the road as it goes over it, whereupon you say, 'Thank
you, ma'am.'

Playing of Rama, and it was the most wonderful thing I ever saw. I guess literature will always be closest to my heart, and when it is put into a dance-drama it penetrates me with no holds barred. The humour and grace of it, the joy in the old stories, the magnificence of the costumes, the sinuous dances, the charming animal dances, but best of all the way they say the verses, lilting, spirited, a combination of the intonation of natural speech and the rhythm and tune of pure music. I have never heard anything like it, and what made it most wonderful was the delight and fervour and intimacy with which they spoke the words; sometimes, hearing poets recite their own poems still in manuscript, or watching Martha Graham demonstrate a step she had just created, I have seen something of that same joyous, bone-deep, captivated spirit. I could have seen that dance-drama a thousand times, but the very next night the director, Jyotirindra Moitra, a friend of Kshitish Roy, came to the house; he was old, with long hair and a woolly vest, and he kept eating spoonfuls of jelly straight from the jar, and he recited the verses with that same amazing feeling but even deeper, as if he was not only the man who wrote the poem, but even the person who originally spoke the lines, Rama himself, or Hanuman, the magical monkey, everyone. And as he spoke he danced the lines with his right hand—I can think of no other way to describe it. Sometimes, with palm upward, he would slice the air, or make sprinkling motions, or, holding the two middle fingers with his thumb in the sign of the hex, he would make a circle, or point to each word he spoke, or throw his hand open, or strike with a fist, but always his

hand seemed to be speaking the word he was uttering. And
I realized that it is not at all artificial, hardly even stylized,
for Indians to invent dances where the hands speak; this
is the way they *do* speak; far more even than an Italian or
a Jew, if you tie a Bengali's hands, he becomes mute. And
the choruses of the Greek dramas, too, seem completely
natural to me now; the way the lines are said, speech blends
into verse, and verse into music, and you can hardly tell
where one stops and the other begins. Jyotirindra Moitra is
now going to Calcutta to work with Satyajit Ray (another
old friend of Kshitish Roy, all of them the boys from
Shantiniketan), but then he hopes to bring the Ramlila to
New York.

Mishtuni and I went to Agra for two days. We stopped
at Mathura, staying at her uncle's house. I think I could
almost make a summary of my tour of India in terms of the
different methods of sewage disposal; in Mathura, you sit
on a kind of potty chair with a metal pot set in it, and after
you're done, a servant comes and empties the pot. It seems
to me that such a system could only persist in the land of
the caste system, but that's the way they do it. When we
bicycled back to Mishtuni's uncle's house (wearing saris,
and that's quite a trick) and went to the bathroom, the
pots were still full, and Mishtuni warned me, 'The cup
runneth over.'

At the Mathura museum we saw some wonderful
things, and wonderful title cards. 'An Eight-handed
Vishnu' (a new kind of poker game, perhaps), 'Amorous
Woman Playing with Balls', 'Rsi Srnga in Ecstasy at his
first experience of sex' (this is really a lovely statue, with

a wonderful story behind it, but too much to tell now[*]), 'Relief Showing Some Scene' (an orgy, some scene indeed), and 'Relief Showing the Extinction of Buddha'. There is also a statue which settles a long argument I've been having with Ingalls, as to whether Kinnaras have horse heads and human bodies or vice versa: this Kinnara had the head and breast of a woman, and the hind quarters of a horse, but her mate was vice versa.[†]

Before we had gone to Agra, Mishtuni's father had read us a translation he was just publishing of Rabindranath's famous poem about the Taj Mahal. First he extols its beauty and eternity, 'a tear on the cheek of time', but then he says that Shahjahan is more wonderful than the building he had built; the building is memory, static, eternal, but Shahjahan, like love itself, has gone forward, changing into another form of life, more wonderful than the perfection of stone. It is a wonderful poem, and I thought of it when I saw the Taj (by sunlight, unfortunately, as we missed the full moon), and I found it very full of death, and cold, though the marble is more liquid than any stone could be, and the dome seems to swell as you look at it. We then saw the tomb of Akbar, which moved me far more deeply; in the centre of a most magnificent, inlaid, marble, elaborate mausoleum, fit for an emperor of Akbar's might, a staircase leads down to the room where his coffin lies—and it is an absolutely bare, plain, cold room, with a marble box of bones in the centre, and the thin light from one narrow

---

* I told it at some length in *Siva: The Erotic Ascetic*.

† This is a theme that I discussed in *Winged Stallions and Wicked Mares*, in 2021.

Mishtuni Roy at the Taj Mahal.

window in the east. I have always loved Akbar, but most at
that moment, when he expressed the mortality of empire
more stunningly than I have ever known.

Then we saw the fort at Agra. I have come to understand
for the first time, seeing the endless fields and the beautiful
women and the wonderful Arabian horses and the shining
brass pots everywhere, just why the Arabs and so many
others always wanted to possess India. Before, that desire
just seemed foolish to me, and full of the stupidity of
politics, but now I see it as the real lust that it must have
been. To possess India—and yet possession is a spirit so
completely alien to the Indian spirit, and perhaps that is
why it was so easy for such a small band of outsiders—first

the Arabs, then the British—to conquer and rule so many million Indians. When I saw the tremendous Mughal fort, it seemed like such a brutal thing, and it was an amazing revelation for me to go inside, and sense once again, but on a far more personal level, what it was that made them fight so fiercely to retain it.

Inside the fort was the most beautiful, delicate, lively green miniature city, a full life. First the steep stone hill where the horses galloped home, and above it the palaces where the women must have stood to see if their husbands had come home alive this time. Then, at the top of the hill, a green field, with shade trees and wells, and a quiet white mosque above it, and places where the goats and sheep used to graze, and the children played. I think the men, standing at the narrow slits of the fortress walls, must have been able to smell the cooking of the women in the palaces behind them, and perhaps hear their children's voices shouting at play, and the sound of the women praying for them in the mosque only a few hundred feet above them on the hill, as they shot their long bows at the attacking enemy. I could see windows in the palaces that looked out upon the moat below, and I could really understand how these soldiers would fight to the death when they had their whole life right there behind them, put to the sword. It reminded me of the chapter in the *Iliad* when Achilles gets ready to fight, and he takes up the great shield that Hephaestus had made for him, and on that shield are pastoral scenes, and battle scenes, and villages, and palaces—all of Greek life is there, staked upon Achilles's battle. And I remember reading what one of the Mughal kings had said about Agra: 'If there is a

heaven upon earth, it is here, it is here, it is here.* And I *felt*
it as heaven upon earth, as the most precious place in the
world. And in a part of one of the palaces, Shahjahan was
kept prisoner, but the room was so exquisite, so majestic, so
delightful, I could only think that in India they realize that
a king is always a king, and treat him so even in captivity,
quite unlike the hideous dungeons where the European
kings were kept.† Of course, these same Mughals were in
the habit of murdering all their brothers,‡ 'so that there
should arise no dispute over the kingdom', but still, if they
let them live at all, they really let them live.

I went to Vrindavan, where Krishna played his childish
pranks on Radha and the gopis and made love in the woods
at night, and it was quite a big disappointment. Now there
is just a scrubby village and a modern temple. I wanted to
go into the temple. First, they said that they had just fed
the god and I had to wait until he had finished eating (at
which time his leftovers are fed to the people); then they
had to know whether Mishtuni or I were menstruating (if
we had been, we couldn't have entered); and finally, after
all that, I couldn't enter because I am a *mlechchha* (non-

---

* The line is generally ascribed to Jahangir, who is said to have said it not
about Agra but about Kashmir: *Gar Firdaus ruhe zamin ast, hamin asto hamin
asto hamin ast.* But see the excerpt from Rana Safvi's book *Shahjahanabad*
(2019) that appeared on Scroll.in (https://scroll.in/article/942273/who-
really-wrote-the-lines-if-there-is-paradise-on-earth-it-is-this-it-is-this-
it-is-this/, last accessed on March 23, 2022).

† Another wildly inaccurate historical generalization. Mary Queen of Scots,
to name just one of the most famous, was kept in relative comfort (going
out to ride horses, attending banquets) for some nineteen years—and was
then beheaded.

‡ Just Aurangzeb; hardly a family habit.

Hindu), which they might have told me in the first place. I had a similar experience in a shop where I asked the price of a tiger skin. The man said the price would depend on whether the skin was mounted or not mounted. I said I wanted one not mounted, and after a long time he said, 'We only have them mounted.'

So Vrindavan was a letdown, but no real place can ever live up to Paul Tripp's old Imagi Nation.[*] Art is always more wonderful than the reality it tells about—except, perhaps, the art that depicts sex, and I guess that's why people keep on trying to depict it, more in India than anywhere else, because they never can capture it. I suppose, really, all sense experience eludes the grasp of art, but Indian literature comes closer to it than any that I know and adds a dimension of divinity that transforms every sense impression into a mental image of overpowering magnitude. And so the things that have exceeded my expectations here are the art, the beauty of nature, and the charm of the people, but I have not yet learned to find divinity in all the strange places that the Indians do. Perhaps it is not in me to find divinity at all, and I will have to settle for nature, and next to nature, art (like the Dying Philosopher[†]).

---

[*] 'Mr I. Magination' was a children's radio programme, starring Paul Tripp, that I used to listen to back in the 1940s.

[†] William Savage Landor, 'Dying Speech of an Old Philosopher':
I strove with none, for none was worth my strife.
Nature I loved, and next to nature, art.
I warmed both hands before the fire of life.
It sinks, and I am ready to depart.

23 A. *Miscellaneous travel notes, undated*

There are many wonderful things in the South Indian temples. Not the least wonderful is a group of nineteenth-century statues of women in the act of worshipping an enormous phallus, and the face of one of the women is absolutely a dead ringer for Victoria. To me, this was the ultimate revenge; the Indians have gotten back some of their own, and Victoria must be spinning in her grave, to be immortalized worshipping such an unamusing* thing. (It occurs to me that lingam worship would go over pretty big in the United States these days if we could get the Madison Avenue boys behind it.)

It surprised me to see how closely the Vaishnava and Shaiva sects have come together since the period of medieval opposition. In the Lingaraja temple of Bhubaneshwar, both Shaivas and Vaishnavas worship, and also in the great Benares temple (the Vishwanatha). In one Shaiva temple I saw the avatars of Vishnu depicted on the inner dome, and when I asked the priest, 'Is this a Vaishnava temple?' and he said no, and then I pointed out the avatars, he said, 'Oh, that's just for decoration.' When you think what religious fanatics some Indians are, and then try to imagine a cross in a synagogue 'just for decoration', it really means something, and you wonder about the priest's statement.

The erotic temples at Bhubaneshwar are very lovely, very shy compared to Konark. The more modest couples perform the deed of darkness in little niches hidden behind

---

* Queen Victoria is said to have said, when a dinner guest told an off-colour story, 'We are not amused.' The anecdote was told by Caroline Holland in *The Notebooks of a Spinster Lady* (1919).

things, to give them privacy, with the two-backed beast
popping out in the most unexpected places, while the larger
and more easily visible sculptures are more controlled.
Usually I have little patience and imagination for art work
that has been broken by the ravages of time, headless statues
and faded paintings, but here I found the very dilapidation
of the temples moving. It seems especially wonderful that
a couple in which his head is missing and her foot broken
off and the fingers made indistinguishable by the wind can
still project such a powerful and subtle feeling of passion
and tenderness just through the tensions in the body. Most
of the statues are intact, and I guess that helps to imagine
the broken ones, but all of it is right there in the stones.

There is wonderful art in Bombay, too, best of all the
Elephanta caves, carved right out of a mountain on a small
tropical island, and all of the sculptures monolithic and
enormous. The size really makes a difference, and gives
you a feeling that I for one can't get from the photographs
I've seen of the caves, a feeling of divinity and tremendous
natural forces. All the carvings are scenes from the life of
Shiva, with Parvati always by his side complementing his
mood, jealous of him when he flirts with the Ganges, shy
when he takes her hand in marriage, respectful when he
is practising yoga, and even playing chess with him in one
scene. There was such delicacy and subtlety and tenderness
in it, and yet, because of the size (and really size in the
plastic arts sets the mood much as the key does in music),
awe-inspiring. The Bombay museum has a marvellous
collection of Indian miniatures; the Rajput paintings have
surrealistic skies like Van Gogh's or Nolde's, and symbolic

skies, blood red for the background of a lady impassioned or an elephant in rut. And there was a lovely one of Krishna supposedly milking a cow, but his eyes are hypnotized upon the form of Radha bathing nearby... I went to a temple nearby, and started taking off my shoes, but the man at the door said, 'This is a ruined temple. There is no god in it. You do not have to take off your shoes.'

Unless one is very thick-skinned, it is difficult to live in India. There is beauty everywhere, but most of it is no longer a part of the people, and the people are very sad. You can't escape it even if you try. I visited some ancient Jain caves outside of Bhubaneshwar on the top of a mountain, with the air thin and the sound of temple horns far away, and a monk humming contentedly as he gave the incense and flowers to the god; an old woman climbed the hill with me, carrying an offering, walking laboriously, and as she reached the top and entered the shrine she took a deep breath and said in a voice like an invocation, 'Om, Devi!' which is really just, 'Hello, God.' I took the peaceful feeling of it away with me as I scrambled down the mountain.

But on the way back to the town I began to talk to the rickshaw walla, and it was such a sad story. He had gone to war, then his whole family was killed during the Japanese bombings; he came back to India, had a job in a hotel in Calcutta (he is well enough educated to be something much more than a rickshaw walla), had a family, but then his only son died of smallpox, and he had to leave Calcutta, and since then he doesn't care about anything and just drives a rickshaw. Almost everyone in India has a story like that to tell. (There is a famous story about the Buddha: A woman whose children had all died went to the Buddha for solace; he gave her a pitcher and said, 'Give this pitcher to someone in whose family there has been no sorrow, and your sorrow will disappear.' She went from house to house, but of course in each house there was sorrow, and then she understood and went about living again.) And this makes for identity crises of the highest order. I love beautiful things, and find them here, but I feel guilty in enjoying them in the midst of such oppression; I want to do something about the beggars, but there is nothing to be done except by the Indian people themselves; you can give to them, of course, but it is a bottomless pit, and you cannot give even enough to salve the conscience, let alone enough for all. Sometimes I feel that it is worth all the suffering to produce such beautiful ideas and images, even if only a few can enjoy them, and then one glance at a hungry child and all that aristocratic sophism falls in. It makes for terrible ambivalence. I live a Spartan life here, and would feel heartless to do otherwise, yet I am aware of the way I really *am*, and that isn't Spartan, so I save up all the beautiful things I find, and cherish the beautiful thoughts that I have come upon, because I know that once I return to my own element I will be, as always, eclectic, guarding the wheat and ignoring the chaff, and especially so about India, where there is such a vast gulf between the sublime and the ridiculous. This may not be hypocritical, but it certainly is schizophrenic, and I find it difficult to come to terms with it, especially living in the middle of it, where the Indian people themselves are undergoing a revolution in values with, I think, deeply destructive results.

Well, more cheerful random notes. On their cards and doorplates and stationery, many Indians put their college degrees, but they do it even when they don't graduate; still, they are scrupulously honest, and you see cards with 'S.K. Chatterjee, BA failed'. My very favourite is one which means that they flunked out even before the final exams came up: 'BA plucked'.

Someday I will write an article on Indian hotels. Every night they ask you what time in the morning you will want your 'bed tea', and you say (if you're me), 'Nine o'clock,' and every morning at seven sharp there is a terrific pounding at the door and they bring you your tea. *Every* time. At even fancy hotels you'll find enormous slugs crawling in the bathtubs, and cockroaches *five* inches long. But this is tame compared to Shantiniketan, where, one evening as I went to the John, I happened to glance into it as I turned around—Indian toilets are just holes in the floor, but with plumbing—and there I saw an enormous black snake looking up at me. I screamed like a banshee, and the *durwan* came and killed him, and it wasn't a poisonous one, but old Freud would have had a field day with the nightmares I had for the next few weeks.[*]

And Indian hotels have a passion for moving you around. At the Oceanic in Madras I was asked to move, so I packed up all my suitcases, expecting to spend the last day in a smaller room, and the bearers came and carried everything away, and then I went to the new room and it was *exactly* the same as the one I had had to leave, even

---

[*] The episode of the snake in the toilet at Shantiniketan must have made a deep impression on me, because I had already narrated it (October 4, 1963).

to the picture on the wall and the layout of the closets and bathroom. Thinking that my room might have been requested by a returning honeymoon couple for old time's sake, or had to be searched for diamonds hidden in the lighting fixture, I asked at the desk. But no, they had simply written down that number for a guest coming in, so they had to give him that number. And since then it has happened to me several times.

I have discovered one thread in Indian religion that interests me very much. It is the role of the human god. Starting with Indra, who commits every sin and grows greatly by it; and then Damayanti who loved Nala, and chose him, when the four gods took his identical form alongside him, because she could recognize him by the sweat on his brow, the dust on his body, the blinking of his eyes, and the shadow and the touching of his feet on the ground (none of which are present in gods[*]), and she *preferred* the human being with those faults; then the story of the woman who married the sun but couldn't stand him until some of his glory had been trimmed away;[†] and of course Krishna, who stole butter and danced with the cowherds' wives; and my old pal Shiva, who is always being cursed by the sages because he goes around with a tremendous lingam, and drinking wine;[‡] and a parallel tradition with a real person, Chaitanya, a seventeenth-century Bengali saint, who taught that every human being is a god—all of this has never been put together, and it intrigues me,

---

[*] This is a myth that I discussed at length in *Splitting the Difference*.

[†] Saranyu again, discussed in *Splitting the Difference* and in *Winged Stallions*.

[‡] In *Siva: The Erotic Ascetic*.

and I find more and more of it in the mythology as I look for it.[*] The love of human faults in a god is something I feel a personal sympathy for—I've always disliked Christ for his lack of them, and liked Zeus and Wotan for them, and Jehovah, too, for losing his temper and sulking, and going back on his word. This is the way the gods *are*; 'like wanton boys with flies, they kill us for their sport' [in Shakespeare's *King Lear*]. It has its horrible aspects as well as its charming ones, but it strikes me, moves me, as *true*, and I want to find out more about it.[†]

Random notes: People always say that it's amazing the way the Indians live so well on a vegetarian diet. Well, they don't, they all suffer from malnutrition, even the rich ones, and in every single house I visit there is always a room where one person is in bed with a high fever.

We gave a lift to a man when we were driving to Vrindavan, and when he got out he said, in English, 'You have obliged me with your sympathetic action.' I love Indian English; it is full of surprises.

I keep seeing signs like, 'Vote for S.K. Govind', which is like 'Vote for Jesus'.[‡] The voting signs are funny because of the names, as here the name of almost every man is god, literally as well as figuratively, but it always makes me smile to think how closely religion is tied up in politics here.

I met an American woman married to a Bengali friend of Kshitish Roy, and I never thought it would be music to

---

[*] This was the subject of the paper that I presented at the International Congress of Orientalists (see the letter of February 16, 1964).

[†] A lot of this went into *The Origins of Evil in Hindu Mythology*.

[‡] Govind, 'cow-finder', is a name of Krishna, and as common as a surname in India as 'Jesus' is as a first name in many Hispanic countries.

my ears to hear a Bronx accent, but it was, and she delighted
equally in my New Yorkese. We agreed on all sorts of
things—the disturbing effect of talking to Indian men,
who don't flirt; the advantage of wearing a sari because
people stare at you less when they can't see your legs and
your zippers and things—we just talked and talked, and
it did us both great good to find that we liked each other
for qualities that we valued in ourselves but had no place
to put in India, kinds of wit and values that are simply
nonsensical to any Indian. She was an ordinary sort of girl,
and she kept saying 'My husband' in the same intense way
that Mrs Roy had spoken of her husband, desperate but
full of tremendous pride and the knowledge that, though
it might be challenged every minute of the day, the choice
was so right and so inevitable as to be hardly called a choice
at all. Still, I could feel her homesickness, and I know she
felt mine.

24. November 22, 1963,
Delhi

I'm glad I'm going back to Calcutta. Delhi is the epitome
of the India I like least, the India that is ashamed of
being India and wants to be America. Most of the city is
tastelessly modern, inhabited by non-Indian diplomats and
businessmen. The whole city is geared to Europeans. In
the post office I was given deferential treatment, put at the
front of the line, cowtowed* to. Everyone speaks English.
In Calcutta, I now realize, there is still enough provincial

---

* I should have spelled this 'kowtowed', but in the Indian context, perhaps
cowtowed is better

pride and independence for the people to treat non-Indians as equals, or frequently inferiors, and if you couldn't speak Bengali you just weren't bothered with. I *much* prefer this. Delhi is all snake-charmers and tourist emporiums and small ivory models of the Taj Mahal. On the other hand, it is not nearly as filthy, poor, and crowded as Calcutta, and when I first arrived in Delhi and hated the place on sight, I suddenly began to be angry with myself, to wonder if I had the right to wish the people of India to be miserable just so that I could find them picturesque. For most Indians (even some Bengalis, though usually not) admire and crave the modern life. What book is it in which the Englishman muses that someday all his children, all the world, may be Americans? I feel that we are only partly responsible, however; it is the duty of the educated in India to pick and use only the good which we have to offer. The Bengalis have picked Yeats* and Coca-Cola; the Delhians [sic], flush toilets and air-conditioning. And it has really gone too far; now they are introducing television and space probes, while in the old part of Delhi people live in the streets. But some of the Indian writers are beginning to realize the value of what they have thrown away; articles appear bemoaning the fact that India is trying so hard to do what other nations do better and has no pride in her own way of life. And here too the British have a subtle guilt; the government officials, British-trained and culturally castrated, have been separated from the Indian tradition and make no place for it in their educational and economic plans. I refuse to

---

* Not exactly an American, but I seem to have switched in this sentence to non-Indian culture more broadly conceived.

believe, as some argue, that it is impossible to preserve diversity if everyone is to have enough, that it is necessary to mass produce to produce enough. In the villages, and even in Calcutta, those who have advanced economically have still preserved their customs of painting their houses, wearing their native dress, reading their own literature, and even the poor people eat off beautiful metal plates that last for centuries, while in Delhi everyone prefers plastic that is certainly less economical in the long run, but it's 'American' and so preferred. The pity of it is that the rich and educated here are the worst of all; when Santha Rama Rau, in a BBC interview, was asked to 'say something in Sanskrit for the lady', she at first hesitated, as I thought out of indecision as to *what* to say, to choose, but when the BBC finally got her back to the wall, she mumbled some meaningless syllables. And then she said that there was nothing of value in Indian literature since the Vedas, 'except,' she added as an afterthought, 'those four novels of R.K. Narayan.' When she comes out with things like this, it's little wonder that the others are flocking to rock and roll and god knows what else. And I really think the West has done them little good. Only in the cities are there beggars (there are poor people in the villages, but they have too much pride to beg; it would never occur to them) and filth (Indians everywhere are really the cleanest people in the world, they bathe constantly, but in the cities the water they bathe in is sewage) and people with a complete lack of personal and national pride. In the villages, a non-Indian woman is stared at, but with amusement and curiosity and friendliness; in the cities the stares are less obvious (they have been taught that it is rude to stare, which is of course ridiculous; it's perfectly natural and harmless to stare, as long as the staree doesn't think it rude to stare) but are filled with envy and hatred and distrust. This is what we have done to them, and it makes me wonder if after all this we have the right to make them stay *beautiful* if they don't want to. But I know I can't help wanting to. I feel like a parent of a child who has lovely long hair, and she wants to cut it off because her friends all have crew cuts; I simply cannot bear to let her do it, but I love her, and she wants a crew cut.

I just found out that the temples of Madurai, perhaps the most intricate and magnificent in all of India, have been, on government order and funds, painted bright, shiny blue, which, aside from its astounding hideousness, has incidentally masked all the details of the soft stone, filling in all the sharp spaces with thick, shiny paint. This of course is sheer stupidity, but sometimes there is a human cost in the preservation of ancient glories. This was brought sharply home to me when I learned that the Ancient Fort [Purana Qila], whose ruins are scattered so strikingly and excitingly throughout Delhi, had housed thousands of refugees in its main citadel (rather appropriate that refugees from Pakistan should live in the Mughal ruins, but pitiful all the more) and at last the police came and just drove them all out like sheep, like bees smoked out of an old barn, and the people, carrying their belongings in small bundles, wandered around the city trying to find alleys in which to lie down and sleep and cook. The government decided to use the citadel as a tourist shrine, as I guess it really ought to be, but what about all the people living in it? And when they *do* try to build new 'modren' houses they are crippled by the very clinging Indianism which I so love: for instance, they can't build developments any more than two storeys high,* because in the hot season the people on the first floor go and sleep in the garden and the people on the second floor sleep on the roof, and no one will take the third storey because where would they sleep in the hot season? And these new houses are hideous and unsuited for the climate and generally a failure, one of those things that India just cannot do as well as other nations. But they *need* houses. I really can't sort it out in my mind; perhaps I will understand it better later on.

Well, Delhi is a Muslim town anyway, and being a Hindu I was glad to leave it. I went to see the Qutb Minar ruins and was unimpressed until I happened to see that some of the stones used in building the walls were carved stones from Hindu temples, and these stones just sprang out from the arid Muslim architecture, so much more alive, lovely figures, laughing at the Mughals who worked so hard and still couldn't match the beauty of the Hindu leftovers which they carelessly tossed into their walls. The Mughals really never understood India, and in their architecture, even the most beautiful—and some of it *is* beautiful—I get the same feeling of unsuccessful transplant that I get from the Levittowns of Delhi and the fragile modernism of Le Corbusier's Chandigarh, which sits in the middle of Punjab like a cubist ostrich hiding its head in the Indian sands. The

---

* This may or may not still have been true in 1963, but it was certainly not true for long.

Taj, for instance, is marvellous, but it belongs in a Persian garden, not in the irregular splendour of the plains of Agra. The sharp silhouette of the dome, the insolent whiteness of the marble, the delicacy of the minarets—these are fighting a constant battle with the landscape, instead of melting into it and rising out of it the way the Hindu temples do. In photographs, the Hindu temples look a little silly and sort of bulgy, but in India they are breathtaking. They melt into the land like tigers in the jungles, grasshoppers on leaves. They are of the colour of the land, and the shape of the land, and, in fact, of the very substance of the land, sandstone and granite, not perilously imported marble. Sometimes, as in Ellora, they are actually *in* the land,* but always they belong there, quiet and indisputable, firmly entrenched, secure, like the earth-bound, flexible, surging motions of Indian dance, so unlike the air-borne, delicate poised motions of ballet. They rise out of the landscape like great contorted rocks or trees, or settle on the tops of the hills like still another peak, and the sculptures on them are vibrant and swarming like the rows of fungus on the trees, or the vertical twistings of the banyan roots, like pieces of crazy driftwood, or the magic cliffs at Bryce Canyon, whistled into strange shapes by desolate winds. And inside, they're dark and wet like jungles, with faces smiling out from under shadows, floating across the ceilings like dark clouds, growing up the walls. They are made of gods, as well as being the houses of gods.

---

* Here I am thinking of the Kailasanatha temple at Ellora, which is carved down into the rock so that the highest pinnacle of the temple is at ground level.

And the same contrast exists between the Mughal
forts and the Hindu forts. The Mughal forts, like the
one at Agra, are rough and hideous on the outside, but
inside are the gardens and delicate mosques, like pearls
within the gnarled shells of oysters. But the Hindu fort at
Chittorgarh has carved figures and shrines scattered even
along the wall itself, softening and humanizing its strong
lines, while the palaces within are as rugged as the walls
are gentle, so that you can hardly tell where the fortress
ends and the living quarters begin. It blends in perfectly,
and yet it isn't static; the quality that allows it to remain at
peace with the landscape is its very violence, that matches
the violence of the land.

Inside the Hindu palaces, though, there is a splendour
far more exciting than the sumptuous detail of the Muslim
palaces. The most beautiful of all is at Udaipur. There are
several temples to different gods actually attached to the
palaces; some of those kings needed a lot of luck and a lot
of blessings, and they played both ends against the middle.
I followed their wise example and whenever I entered a
temple I offered a few pennies to the god (in India, even
the gods are poor, and don't turn up their noses at a few
pennies) and accepted from the presiding Brahmin the spot
of paint which he applied to my forehead (*Wenn man der
gibt, nimm...*). The temples are carved in marble and set
with gold, with imported brass statues and embroidered
robes. There are rooms where the domed ceiling is set with
mirrors and tinted glass, so that in the darkness, a candle
waved across the room brings out thousands of swaying
lights in the dome. There are rooms where the walls are

covered with inlays of glass bubbles containing the mosaic flowers that we associate with Venetian glass, but which are made in India, too, covering the whole walls, thousands of them, each different. My favourite room is one, fairly large, where every inch of the walls and domed ceiling is covered with Indian miniature paintings, painted right on the wall like a mural, but instead of a single mural, thousands of miniatures, some a few inches square, some yards long, depicting scenes from Indian literature, court ladies, holy places in India, battles, all of Indian life, each painting with its own illuminated border, laid end to end with the next painting, and each one exquisite. I could spend my life in that room and still not see everything in it, just living in a painting, like the children in *Mary Poppins* walking into Bert's painting on the sidewalk, and if I had to choose the world I wanted to walk into, that wall at Udaipur would be my dream.

Then there was a room, an enclosed balcony really, where each wall was enclosed in glass of a different colour, so that the queen could sit there and look out upon the countryside, the city below, the lake with the palace on an island in the centre, the mountains rising behind the lake, and in one moment she could see it at any time of day she liked, like the series of paintings Monet did of the change of light on the Cathedral and on the haystacks: a rosy light for sunrise, a pale blue glass for full moonlight (and full moonlight in India is an amazing thing, and that pale blue glass window in daylight captures it exactly), a golden glass for late afternoon sun, and a dark, grey-blue glass for the monsoon. At the very top of the palace is a lush garden and a marble swimming pool, to be filled with perfumed water poured from golden pitchers. And here the Indian kings had an area in which to express their luxury that the kings of Europe never knew, a luxury more delicious than all the food and painting and music and silks of all the courts in the world: they could become cool, they could enjoy cool water, and the exquisite pleasure in this is impossible to imagine except after enduring an Indian heat wave (lasting, of course, from March through October). The kings had pools with water pouring from the trunks of marble elephants; they built marble screens, and had cool water poured down them with fans working behind them, driving the moist air through the curved spaces in the marble into the chambers within. It almost seemed like a joke that India was playing upon her kings, that in the midst of all the inconceivable man-made splendour, cool water was still the most splendid thing of all.

I left Udaipur then, and went to Khajuraho, which was far more wonderful than I ever dreamed. It is set in a wonderful landscape, a desert, bare, with a way of highlighting objects in the foreground different from the moist glow of the Bengal air, but vivid and dramatic in its own way, and with trees and gardens relaxing and enlivening the land around the temples. We reached Khajuraho at sunset, which is always a miraculous time of day in India, even in the cities, where it softens and warms and brings forward all surfaces facing west, leaving all the others dark, picking out the tall, western surfaces with a liquid, slanting light that makes everything look two-dimensional, like a stage set, as if there *were* only that one, illuminated side of each building. At Khajuraho, it was more unreal than ever, for a city of temples rises out of nowhere in the middle of the plain, and with the golden light blazing behind them, and red clouds swarming over them, it is breathtaking. All around the temples, which are carved out of a golden, warm sandstone, there is bright green grass and purple bougainvillea and red hibiscus. Squirrels run over the roofs, and pigeons make seductive noises inside, invisible, so that it seems that the couples in the stone outside are moaning to each other. And there was absolutely no one there at all, not a sound, not a whisper but the whisper of the leaves of the palm trees. The figures are larger than I had thought, most of them five feet tall, and there are more of them, and more varied, than the photographs I had seen had led me to expect. And they are not naked; one or two of the women are taking off their lower garments, exposing the navel, which is much deeper and fleshier than the navels on the other women, who are wearing clinging, transparent garments, lending a quiet air to their bodies. And the temples are not at all erotic, seen whole. The coupling figures are just one part of the unity of life, as complex and complete as the life painted in miniatures on the room in Udaipur. Women bathing, mothers with children, animals, demons, gods, flowers, a circus, a wrestling match, a battle, a stubborn mule, an angry elephant, dogs barking—everything is there. And even in the mating figures there is a relaxation and warmth, a gentleness that just melts in with the spirit of all the other scenes, a very matter-of-fact, serene attitude (rather like the attitude of the man in charge of the hostel there, who said, with quiet puzzlement, 'I don't understand why people come just to see the sexual scenes'). There is tremendous energy in the figures, but they just seem to be snuggling, rather than making love, and very simply. The much-feted 'acrobatic' poses, people coupling while standing on their heads, men mating with horses, fellatio, and so on, appear in one single, small, insignificant panel of a frieze that depicts a circus, with parading elephants and wrestlers and trained monkeys. I'm sure it's a kind of exhibition orgy, and the Indians considered it just as silly as it seems to me, and meant it as a joke (there are some wonderful jokes carved on the temples: pot-bellied Brahmins, crotchety old women, mischievous monkeys). Contrary to the impression given by the books, there are many wonderful sculptures of men as well as women, and the Shiva statues are not violent and with erections, like many in other temples, but smiling and relaxed, naked with the sleepy eroticism of Michelangelo's Adam. Gods float across the tops of the temples and lurk in the corners inside, and the stone has a soft glow and golden warmth that makes it seem like young flesh with a peach-bloom over it, firm and rippling. It is so alive, and so joyous, and so glorious, that it bathes you in a feeling of the presence of gods, like the pervading warmth of a sunbath.

One of the reasons that Khajuraho is so delightfully deserted is that it takes some twenty-four hours of train and bus rides, with ill-timed and complicated changes, to get there, but I loved the travelling, once I got used to being constantly sleepy (the trains stop every few minutes each night, and at each stop there is great shouting and commotion, and people violently rattle the doors of your compartment trying to get in) and filthy (the trains burn coal, and travel through deserts, and everything is coated with thick layers of grime in a few minutes) and hungry (nothing but bananas and rice and tea is edible and relatively sanitary).

But what wonderful things to see, especially from the buses and wandering around during the hours between trains. At dawn everyone goes to the fields all together, squatting like rabbits dotted over the hills, thoughtfully contemplating the passing buses as they move their bowels. It's still cool in the early morning, and they wrap long scarves around their bodies and heads and arms, walking around muffled up. The women carry pitchers of water on their heads to the wells, and then the wells are started; this is done by hitching a pair of bullocks to one end of the rope, the other end of which is tied to a great leather bag which is lowered into the well. The bullocks are slowly driven away from the well, pulling up the bag, which is then emptied into the voluptuous brass pots; the bullocks are unhitched, the bag dropped back in, the bullocks are led back to the well, rehitched, and it starts again.

All along the road there are big black-faced monkeys, and lines of smug camels, and sometimes elephants (an elephant carried me up the hill to the castle at Jaipur, and as far as I'm concerned the Hindu kings can keep *that*), lots of peacocks, crazy hairy wild pigs, deer (I spent a night at a game sanctuary, and saw lots of deer), donkeys, horses, porcupines (sometimes called concubines), and various small fry. What civilization there is, is immediately absorbed: there are pick-up trucks, but they are painted green and covered with flowers, with a great big 'OM' on the front. Rajasthan is a prosperous province, and the women wear their entire family bank accounts in the form of tremendous, heavy silver ornaments hanging from their ears, nose, neck, upper arms, wrist, waist, and ankles.[*] Each woman must wear fifty or sixty pounds of silver at least, and they just go out that way and dig in the fields. The houses have wonderful tigers and ladies painted on them, and the Rajasthanis paint everything they can get their hands on, especially the really inviting things to paint, like the long, curved horns of the buffaloes (painted red, yellow, and green, while the buffaloes' sides are painted with pink and red and blue circles like drunken leopards), and the sides of the tongas. One woman I saw, though, was without any silver on her at all; she was sitting by the bus stop, crouched on the ground, weeping, and her husband stood above her, not looking at her; she had a bundle of clothes, and I think he must have been sending her away; perhaps she was unable to bear children, or had stolen.

On the train, early in the morning the Indian gentlemen rise and sit cross-legged, chanting the Gita in a mixture of Sanskrit and Hindi, and in the third-class carriages they live a full life; the carriages are mobbed, with people climbing in from the windows and sitting up in the luggage racks and on the floor under the seats (I wonder where they're all going all the time), and people cook and eat and nurse their

---

* These women and their jewellery found their way into my *The Ring of Truth, and Other Myths of Sex and Jewelry* (2017).

children and fight and sew and change their clothes. The buses are crazy, too: often they drive right past somebody frantically waving them to stop, standing by the road with their little cloth bundle, still waving numbly as the bus goes right by. But, on the other hand, the bus will go several miles off the main road to take a passenger to the particular place he wants to go. As the bus nears a town, little boys run alongside and hang onto the windows, offering to carry your luggage or sell you some oranges.

Driving in a bus up the mountain to Mount Abu was quite an experience. It was after seeing Udaipur, and I kept fearing that I would literally fulfil Max Mueller's injunction to 'see Udaipur and die'.* The road to Abu goes along steep cliffs, unfenced, and the bus has to swing pretty far out in order to get around the hairpin turns. It's only wide enough for one car, so he sometimes blows his horn going around corners, but to do this he has to take a hand off the wheel. The road is slippery with cow dung and often you have to swerve to avoid the monkeys leaping over each other's heads, playing with the baby monkeys. Near the top, after a dizzying, terrifying, steep two-hour ride, the bus stopped at a shrine to Ganesh, to whom we all offered our thankful pennies, as we did once again before starting down again.

I have seen some magnificent Jain temples, but the most wonderful is Mount Abu. The entire temple is carved out of marble, with hundreds of pillars, each with hundreds of panels, each with hundreds of figures (like the man who

---

* Goethe famously remarked, 'See Naples and die.' A variant about Udaipur, 'See Udaipur and live,' is variously attributed to Max Mueller and Rudyard Kipling. I seem to have combined them.

wasn't going to St Ives*). And the most wonderful thing is that every single figure is different, and beautiful, some really exquisite. It struck me that there must be hundreds of millions of hours of work in that temple, and that it represents the entire lifespan of thousands of men. It's a kind of replacement for the bloodier kind of human sacrifice, still sacrificing the life to god, but in a beautiful way, turning transient life into eternal marble, giving oneself to god in a useless, and therefore artistic way. Here there is no need to slaughter a virgin to bury under the altar,† for the man who has carved the statues of the virgins on the altar has sacrificed his youth just as surely.

In another marble Jain temple, in Chittorgarh, I went in, taking off my shoes, basking in the golden sunlight on the white marble (for the temple is mostly without a roof), when I saw a young Jain monk dressed in a red dhoti, the only colour in all the temple, like the spot of red in a Corot, carrying a lamp from idol to idol, and all the time humming a lovely song, sometimes sad, sometimes lively, depending on the character of the god that he was standing before at that moment, like the violinist in a nightclub playing a special request for each table that he approaches, very eager to please, and obviously singing mainly because he liked to sing. I stayed there for a long time watching him, and only went away when he had given the last of his

---

* A riddling joke: 'As I was going to St Ives, I met a man with seven wives. Each wife had seven sacks; each sack had seven cats; each cat had seven kits. Kits, cats, sacks, and wives, how many were going to St Ives?' Answer: One, me.

† It was sometimes alleged that the Hindus buried a sacrificed victim under the cornerstone of a temple.

flowers to the last of the idols and taken off his red dhoti in exchange for the white one that he would wear all day (the red one is just for the sunrise worship). He didn't seem to notice me at all.

Coming out of the temple, still dazzled by its whiteness, I saw a cart drawn by two great big snow-white bullocks, and lying on the cart were three men, in white dhotis and white scarves around their shoulders, with white beards, lying absolutely motionless, silent, their heads propped up on their elbows, jogging slightly from side to side with the slow motion of the bullocks who bumped along, chewing disgustedly and flicking the flies away.

Neither buses nor trains run anywhere near on schedule, of course, and I now know at least one cause for the delay in the trains. Waiting for the train at Harpalpur, the station master invited us to his house, next door to the station, to have tea with his family. We were grateful but expressed concern that we might miss our train. He was astonished. 'I am the station master,' he said. 'The train can't go until I say so.' Sure enough, we had tea, the train arrived, he insisted that we have another cup of tea, kept the train waiting, brought us to it and put us on it. Then he blew his whistle and the train left, late.

All through Rajasthan people were wonderful to us. A man we met on the train in Jaipur turned out to be the head of the forest department, and arranged for our trip to his game sanctuary, and even planned a tiger kill for us. When we arrived, there was a big sign saying, 'Tiger Showing a Speciality of This Sanctuary', but the warden sadly told us, 'The tiger will not come to the tiger kill. He has gone to the mountains for four or five days,' just as if the tiger had discussed his plans with him. And who knows, maybe he had; he didn't come that night. So we had to settle for deer and blue bulls (the blue bulls of Rajasthan go ding dong, etc.*). But the deer alone were well worth the price of admission ($2 for a room and three meals); they came right up to us and paid no attention to us, stretching back their heads to eat leaves, like the deer in the Mughal miniatures, and bounding slowly away after their friends.

At Humayun's tomb [in Delhi] I was guided by a man who turned out to be one of the main actors in the Ramlila that I loved so much, and he told me all sorts of fascinating tales of the Indian stage, also many an apocryphal tale of the history of Humayun [a Mughal emperor] and refused to accept any money from me. It's amazing what a difference that makes here. Half the people have their hands out constantly, just considering Americans people to be cheated, and even though you know how poor they are it eventually gets on your nerves to be treated that way, and you get wary of any profession of friendship until you know how much it's going to cost you. But there are just as many people, like the ones I met in Rajasthan, who simply want to help you out because you're a foreigner, and who want you to like their country, and want you to be their friends. They ask for your address and give you theirs, and promise to write. And they are just as poor as, or poorer than, the ones who just want to see what they can get from

* A pun on 'The brown bells of Merthyr' in 'The Bells of Rhymney', a song that Pete Seeger used to sing.

you. But they're ashamed of the money-grubbers, and try to make up for it. Most of the nice ones are in the country, the not nice ones in the city, but it isn't a strict division.

In one village I had several hours before train time, and some fifteen shots left on a roll of black and white film I had used at Khajuraho and wanted to finish up, and the children in the village had wonderful faces, so I asked one or two of them if I could take their pictures, and pictures of the babies that young children in India carry around like dolls. They were delighted, and before I knew it I was surrounded by hundreds of children begging me to take their pictures; some of them ran home and woke up their baby brothers and ran back with them still half asleep for me to photograph. And an old lady, toothless and jolly, insisted that I take a picture of her standing proudly next to her husband. The whole village was in on it, and I only had trouble trying to explain to them that it takes a while for pictures to be developed; they kept asking to see the pictures right then, and I didn't know whether they just had no concept of a camera or whether some tourist with a Polaroid Land camera had been there before me. India's such a funny place, you just don't know. Indian children have an astonishing beauty. But Brahmins have religious scruples against being photographed. Sometimes I would raise my camera and they would all scream with laughter and I'd know that I couldn't photograph that one; the child would tease me, posing until I focused, then running away and hiding, laughing and laughing.

Part Six

RETURN TO CALCUTTA
AND SHANTINIKETAN

This section opens in Delhi, where I stayed at the Fairbanks' home. Though I promise to tell in 'other letters' how I got there, I never did, nor can I remember it now. But what I did and do remember, and did not tell my parents, was that, on an earlier occasion, Gordon Fairbanks had brought me to the Delhi train station late one night with his young daughter, Connie, who was travelling with me on her first trip away from home; I was taking her with me on one of my trips to Rajasthan. At the station, we discovered that we had been assigned an overnight carriage that had four berths and was, like most Indian trains at that time, accessible only from the side doors, at the train station; there was no corridor, no way in or out of the compartment when the train was in motion. And two of the berths were already occupied by two big, muscular-looking Sikhs, already in their pyjamas, with whom we would be locked in overnight. Professor Fairbanks turned pale, but eventually it transpired that the Sikhs were gentlemen, and knew people that he knew, and they exchanged cards, and he was somewhat reassured. And indeed we travelled in perfect safety.

The letters in this section document a number of final leave-takings, on several different levels. It was in Delhi that I learned of the assassination of President Kennedy, and lovingly recalled his pronunciation of 'Vigah'. (Kennedy had a strong Boston accent, which made him drop some of his final 'r's, pronouncing a final '-er' or '-or' as '-ah'. And, on the other hand, he would add a final 'r' to words that had none, calling Cuba, 'Cuber'.) Here again my political naïveté emerges in my violent condemnation of Johnson, even to the point of suspecting him of complicity in Kennedy's death. But I was not thinking straight at the time, and was talking off the top of my head, as I really knew very little about Johnson then. Equally naïve are my parroted criticisms of Nehru (December 11, 1963), which, as usual, largely reflect Chanchal's tirades.

It was also on this occasion that I saw Mishtuni Roy for the last time in India, though I kept in touch with her by mail after I left India. In 1965, Mishtuni married Anthony (Tony) John Bevins, whom she had met when he was in Bengal, teaching for the Voluntary Service Overseas. They married in a Bengal temple and moved to England, where I saw her on occasion during my years at Oxford (1965–75). They had two children, Rabi and Nandini. Tony Bevins became a famous journalist and politician, the first political editor of the *Independent*; Colin Hughes credited him with bringing down Margaret Thatcher, and the Bevins Prize was named in his honour. In 2001, Tony contracted pneumonia; Mishtuni flew to his side and collapsed on his hospital bed, dead, and Tony died a few days later. Hughes's obituary for Tony Bevins in the *Guardian*, March 25, 2001, included this sentence: 'Tony and Mishtu's searingly honest, openly emotional relationship made for legendary dinners at their home in Cookham, Berkshire, eating the best curry this side of Calcutta, fighting over politics, reciting Tagore aloud in the original over the eau de vie at 4 am.' Apparently some things had never changed since Shantiniketan in 1964.

Chanchal with the Prime Minister of India Lal Bahadur Shastri.

And it was at this time that I also said goodbye to Chanchal, whom I never did meet again. This section of my letters represents some more of Chanchal's highly biased anti-Muslim diatribes. It's not clear to me how much of it I believed then, but I certainly don't believe it all now. In any case, years after Chanchal had died, her son came to visit me in Chicago. And when I had just begun to put this book together and gave a talk about it for the Bengal Club in Kolkata, in June 2021, Chanchal's daughter Rini Debroy was there and we got together and she was able to tell me about the later decades of Chanchal's life. Chanchal did indeed marry a Bengali, but not the one she had known at Shantiniketan; in Chicago, in 1967, she met a Hindu from pre-Partition Bangladesh, an orthopaedic surgeon. They married and lived in the United States until they moved back to India in 1987. Chanchal stopped working when she married and raised their three children, two girls and a boy; one is a paediatrician, one a surgeon. She died of a heart attack in 2008.

In my later work as a scholar, I found that I could read these two strong personalities, Mishtuni and Chanchal, into the equally strong personalities, not of the authors of my Sanskrit texts but of fictional characters in those texts, characters who then became very real to me. The spunkiness of Shakuntala, more in the *Mahabharata* version than in Kalidasa's poem about her; then the courage of Parvati, in both the Puranas and the folk tellings when she talks back to her husband; and going back to Gargi in the Upanishads, who holds her own among all the male scholars—I *knew* those women, and I could imagine their gestures and their facial expressions by remembering the spirited women that I had known at Shantiniketan. That made a big difference in the way I read the texts for the rest of my life.

Though this was the final chapter of those Indian friendships, it was also a time when I connected with a number of other friends, both old friends from the States and newer Indian friends. In Calcutta, I actually bumped into Pete Seeger by chance on the street. I had known him since I was a teenager, as he was a friend of my mother and had taught me my first Sanskrit—the words to 'Raghupati Raghava Raja Ram'. I had often attended Seeger's 'Hootenannies', folk-singing festivals that he made famous, and had heard him sing at the YMCA at 92nd Street in Manhattan, where many poets and folk singers often performed.

In Delhi I met again with Jamini Roy. I refer to him in my letters as 'old', just as I had referred to Hazra and Jyotirindra Moitra. Born in 1887, Jamini would have been seventy-six when I met him. He died nine years later, in 1972. The letters then revert to my Bengali friends, who would often tease me about my mistakes in Bengali. In particular, whenever I didn't know a word I needed in Bengali, I would put in a Sanskrit word and pronounce it with a Bengali accent, as there are actually still quite a lot of Bengali words derived from Sanskrit. But this produced a highfalutin' and pompous register, rather like the affectation of the sorts of people who use a lot of Latin locutions in English; it was a kind of Bengali spoken by pedants and by family priests (called purohits). And so my friends would laugh at me and say, 'Listen to the purohit!'

∽

25. *November 24, 1963,*
c/o Dimock

At six o'clock yesterday morning, when I was asleep [in Delhi] at the home of Gordon Fairbanks, head of the Ford Foundation in India (how I got there is a long story, to be told in other letters), Mrs Fairbanks burst into my room weeping hysterically. As I awoke, I thought that something had happened to her husband, as he was ill, and I was suddenly aware of my heart beating. 'Wendy, Kennedy was killed!' she cried out, and from her voice I still thought that it was Gordon who had died, and finally I realized what she was saying, but I still didn't grasp what it meant. When I finally understood, when I saw the Indian newspaper with 'Kennedy Assassinated' across the page, I could only think, irrationally, that his baby had died, too. I felt that it was a terrible time for me to be away from my country, and

I never before had felt so like an American. Most of the people in Delhi didn't even know about it, and I had to catch an 8 am train to Calcutta, still in a daze.

[Once on the train,] thoughts ran through my head— Dallas, Texas, Lyndon Johnson's state, had he had Kennedy killed, and my God, Lyndon Johnson as President of the United States; and now Goldwater might actually win; it was only Kennedy's sure re-election that we counted on to stop Goldwater; and had Goldwater hired this man to kill Kennedy counting on his Communist affiliations both to act as a smokescreen and to stir enough anti-Communist feelings to get a reactionary elected in 1964? All of this must seem ridiculous to you, but I didn't have the *New York Times* to guide me, or even a single American to talk to.

And I just had to get on the train with people who didn't know, or, worse, didn't care. Well, after twenty-four hours in the train, I arrived at the Dimocks' and finally had someone to talk to, but still no *Times*. Please send me your own thoughts, the thoughts of people in the know, some *New York Times* clippings, James Reston, something to guide me. I'm terribly confused and unsettled by this. My first impulse, yesterday morning, was to telephone you, but of course I couldn't.

I never realized how fond I was of Kennedy; I think I'm mourning for him as a man even more than as a President. He was so young, and clever, and silly in his own way. This evening Ed said something about some kind of Indian painting that was noted for its fullness and vigour, and I thought, 'Vigah,' and I burst into tears. And I'm angry, too, and I don't know who I'm angry at. Wasn't Dallas the town that spat on Stevenson? And my god what a disaster for the civil rights programme, with that ass Johnson in charge, and that vicious Congress will run all over him; even Kennedy had trouble getting things through that reactionary Congress, and Johnson is practically as bad as the Congress itself, if not worse. I'm really sick about it, and I was just getting so hopeful for America, too. But still I feel like fighting, and I'm glad that I'll be home in plenty of time before the next election, and I can do something.

Well, that's off my chest at least, and there are still many things I want to tell you, though it seems sacrilegious. Still, life does go on, and that's a comfort.

The things I wrote to you about [what people are saying about] Nehru are absolutely true, without exaggeration, but—they are true only of Bengal, not at all of Delhi, where he is everyone's best friend. I think some of this can be attributed to the difference in personality and way of life between Bengali and Delhian [sic], but in addition, it comes down to the old question of whose bull is being gored. The Bengalis are angry because Nehru has spent so much money developing Delhi and left Bengal so poor, so this may account for part of it. But in Bengal and Punjab he is hated, and these are important provinces. The reason you haven't heard about it is because the *Times* correspondents stay in Delhi, where the government is, and miss what's going on in rural areas like Punjab and Bengal. It's funny; I just realized: I must have written to you that I feared that Nehru was in danger of assassination, but never in a million years would I have thought that anyone would have even tried to shoot Kennedy, let alone succeed in killing him. Well, that way madness lies.

Now it's the morning of the 25th, and I have had a lovely sleep, secure in my Indian home. I will stay here from now on, with little side trips to Madras and Benares and Bhubaneshwar for a few days each, and I'm very happy about it. It's a real home for me, a family; yesterday the whole bunch of them came down in the jeep to pick me up at the station, and I brought them presents, and there was much rejoicing. And it's a good, safe place to live, where I can get a balanced diet and a full night's sleep and a good doctor if I ever need one. Ed Dimock is really the centre of literary life in Calcutta, which is in its turn the centre of Indian intellectual life; I can do my work here in my bright room (on whose wall I have already hung a tremendous Mughal wall hanging, a painting on cloth, which I bought in Jaipur) and at night I just have to walk into the living room to meet the editor of the Calcutta *Statesman*, the professor of Comparative Literature at Jadavpur University, and a large number of miscellaneous crazy Bengalis, painters, wandering Baul singers, priests, and general folk. I can use my Bengali, and it's just a short walk to Hazra's house. So I have finally come to roost.

I am sending you for Christmas the most wonderful chess set I ever saw. It's crazy looking, but I think the sizes and shapes are such that it will be easy to play chess with it. It's carved of ivory, painted, and the two teams, no mere black versus white, are the armies of Rama and Ravana in the *Ramayana*. Rama is the King, his brother Lakshman is the Queen, and the rest of the men are the monkeys who helped him get to Ceylon to fight Ravana; they formed a bridge holding onto each others' tails. Plain monkeys are the pawns, and monkeys riding on elephants, horses and camels are, respectively, castles, knights and bishops (after all, a bishop is just a monkey riding a camel). The other side is Ravana and his son (the Queen) and various demons. If you think it's silly, just let me remind you that the Indians invented chess so you can't tell them how to make a chess set.

26. *November 28, 1963*,
c/o *Dimock*

For this last month, my life here has been extremely chaotic. I was travelling, and things got all balled up, and I was stranded in Rajasthan for several days (a very pleasant place to be stranded, but a place without my typewriter, without which I am mute) and then of course the assassination and all the post offices were closed.

The climate is such that there are few working hours in the day, and there's so much I want to do here, but I can't help writing long letters; it just irks me to write about something less clearly and less fully than it deserves. You must *assume* that I am healthy, wealthy and wise enough to take care of myself, and my letters must only serve to supplement that image of me by showing that I am also happy, loving, brilliant, creative, witty, charming, literate, observant, and a dutiful daughter.

A few days ago, we all went down to the American Consulate and signed the book of condolences for Kennedy. I know it's a stupid thing to do, but it was all we *could* do, and it made us feel much better. It was quite a moving sight—there were thousands of people there in a long, long line, standing in the sun for two hours to wait to get to the book, all quietly dressed, quietly standing, with the flag at half-mast and draped in black. It was a very American feeling, somehow, because every American in Calcutta must have been there, and formed a silent community from all the people that had been dispersed all over this very foreign city, with Indians all around. And there were Indians there to sign too, many of them, but a funny thing happened to make us feel even more American. We were just supposed to sign our names, because there were so many waiting, and so many books had already been filled, but the Indians all signed their names, addresses, titles, and postal zones, no matter what anyone said, and that is really a typically Bengali thing to do. And so when it came to us, the consul didn't say anything but just looked as if he expected us to understand, and we did, and we just signed our names. But it was terribly sad, with the photograph of Kennedy draped in black, and only the fans moving in that great room, and everyone still looking dazed and confused. I don't think I will ever forget it.

27. December 5, 1963, chez Dimock

Last night we went to see Pete Seeger and he was terrific, all apple-piously American, sang like a bird, all left-wingish, sang 'We Shall Overcome', and generally behaved as if he were at a Hootenanny at the 92nd street Y, while all the time he was out in the middle of the Calcutta Maidan, with the moon rising and the smoke rising from the burning ghats. It was a great evening, and afterwards we went and talked to him and felt very we-happy-fewish.

I'm going to Shantiniketan for two or three days now, just to pick things up and bring them back here to the Dimocks' house, say goodbye to friends, etc. Chanchal and I will still see each other frequently, as she will come to Calcutta, and the formal structures of Shantiniketan can be replaced by Calcutta elements.

From *Indian Etiquette*, preface: 'It is hoped that this will save our society to some extent from the corruption that is slowly creeping into it, due to our association with men and women with whom we would hate to mix but for the official position held by them or their wealth... Indian ladies do not smoke. It is difficult to give up the habit of smoking. So the Indian ladies who have created the habit of smoking should not smoke in public... It will be wrong on your part to say that such and such lady is your friend. When you are very familiar with a lady, you should say that she is thoroughly acquainted with you... No male is allowed to travel in female compartments. In trains in India there is not sufficient protection against theft and robbery. So, while travelling in trains during night time, people generally like to take their female companions into the same compartments with them for the sake of safety.' Re the last item, there are signs in the trains saying, 'Do not give thieves permission to sleep on the floor of your compartment. Do not accept food or drink from strangers; they may be drugged.'

Some gems of Indian English: 'A cold has caught me.' 'If I don't bring food home to my family, and I am their sole support, the whole family will fast.' ('Don't you mean "starve"?' 'In India we call it fasting.') While travelling,

I passed a house with a large sign proclaiming it to be a 'Novel Farm' and I still can't figure out what it was. In every city I went to, people kept saying, 'You must go and see the Jew,' and I had a vision of a famous rabbi or something, until I discovered that this is the Indian pronunciation of 'zoo'. It still puts me off. Discussing Yeats and Indian mysticism, someone called him an ascetic, and I said, 'For an ascetic, he certainly had a lot of mistresses,' and the answer came, 'Yes, that's impressive.'

It appears that the net profit of the Ford Motor Company last year was greater than the total national income of India, and it has been suggested that Nehru sell India to Ford to see if it could be run at a profit. And as for Nehru's unpopularity in Bengal and Punjab, I have discovered that Gandhi himself is also unpopular, and the hatred stems from the Partition, as does so much in modern Indian life; these were the two provinces that were divided, because of their position (according to the government, quoting statistics of Muslim percentages, etc.) or because they were always the two centres of revolution and criticism of the government (according to the Bengalis and Punjabis). Whatever the reason, the Partition dealt a terrible blow to their economy and they have hated Gandhi and Nehru ever since, in Bengal all the more so because they have their own Bengali leaders, notably Subhas Chandra Bose (Netaji), to reverence as the rest of the country honours Gandhi.

A wry note on the persistence of religious sectarianism even in modern intellectual life. The two great living poets of Bengal are Bishnu Dey and Buddhadeb Bose, and there is great rivalry between them and between their followers, who are known respectively as Vaishnavas and Buddhists.

I get a peculiar sense of time, like that when watching the crazy hemlines in old movies, seeing all the Kaisers and Frazers around Calcutta. I haven't seen one in years at home. Petrol is very expensive here, so every single car going anywhere is always full. Taxi drivers always bring two friends with them for the joyride in the front seat. The trams are unbelievably crowded, making New York rush hour subways seem deserted by comparison; people ride on the roof, ducking each time the tram aerial hits a crosswire, and sit on the windows, and hang onto the outside, so that you can't even see the signs on the outside, they're so covered with people swarming like ants over a piece of sugar. And whenever you hire a taxi to take you somewhere far away, like a temple or a lake, somehow the driver's whole family suddenly materializes, wife and five kids, all piling into the car with you, and along the road they stop several times to go to the bathroom by the side, or to worship the idol in a roadside shrine.

I'm still coming across more aspects of the humanization of the Hindu gods, the paper I'm reading at the convention in January. I realize that this is the significance of the many poems about the goddess Parvati being all messed up by making love with Shiva, her hair untidy, her make-up rubbed off, etc. She is, at this time, a human being, fallible, mess-up-able, if you will, just as a human woman when in the ecstasy of love is considered to partake of the divine. In the same way, it struck me that the women in the sculptures at Khajuraho were more beautiful than the heavenly nymphs *because* of their imperfections, just as Nala was more desirable to Damayanti just because of the dust and sweat on him, qualities that distinguished him from the gods. There is a lot more to this, and it's just beginning to fall into place, which I find very exciting.[*]

There is a young girl here at the Dimocks' named Aminah (she must be thirteen, though her father says she is nineteen) who helps care for the children. Yesterday she staggered in, hysterical, badly beaten by her father. It seems that she was married as an infant, but her husband never came back to find her, so she is considered to be unlucky, and her father threw her out on the street to be a whore, and we just found out that she's been sleeping on the roof of this house for the last month, half-starved. Finally, yesterday she went back home, but was just beaten and thrown out again. She's just a little girl, hardly older than Tony [twelve], if that. This is what I mean by saying that living in Calcutta it is impossible to remain aloof from Indian life.

I read that the Chinese in Tibet are making the few Tibetan women that are there (there has always been a shortage of women) 'marry' Chinese men so that, it has been estimated, in fifty years there will be no Tibetans left. I find this a terrifying thing, a kind of insidious genocide that is in its own way as hideous as the Nazi version. It reminds me of the way they exterminate insects in the Southern swamps, by catching and sterilizing the males, then releasing them to mate with the female insects, who

---

[*] These ideas came to fruition in several books, but particularly in *Splitting the Difference* (1999).

mate only once and therefore remain barren even though there are fertile male insects left, and slowly they all die out. This, with the extermination of national culture that I found so sickening in Delhi, is really making me go all sour on the human race. There will be no more Tibetans, no more Indians, no more individuals except for a fast-dying band living in an atmosphere so rarefied as to be eventually unbearable, as it was to the Intellectual in *La Dolce Vita.*[*]

Honest to God, I really think that by the time they get around to blowing up the whole mess no one will even notice it. Not with a bang but a whimper, as the man says.[†] Poor old Aldous Huxley is dead now and the *Brave New World* has been so closely approached by the brave new world that its humour is merely factual reporting now. I really feel that we are fighting a losing battle and I don't see any way out, except perhaps by keeping the wolf away from our own doors at least in our lifetime, by remembering and hanging on and telling our children, like the band of hobos in *Fahrenheit 451*,[‡] who sat by the railroad tracks while all the books burned and recited to each other the books that they had each memorized before the fire. A grim picture, and one that the replacement of an individual like Kennedy by a politician like Johnson does nothing to offset.

I can't bear to end on such a tragic note. After all, Pete Seeger inspired me with faith in human progress, though it wore off just about as soon as his charismatic presence was gone.

---

* A 1960 Federico Fellini film.

† T.S. Eliot in 'The Hollow Men': 'This is the way the world ends...'

‡ Ray Bradbury's 1953 novel.

28. December 11, 1963,
c/o Dimock [and Shantiniketan]

This last week's visit to Shantiniketan, after all the travelling
and excitement, made me love it all the more as a place to
come home to, and as a place that has remained uniquely
Indian in the face of the encroaching modern world. The
glorious climate, with the thin blue air and deep blue sky
and pale golden sunniness in the afternoons, the constant
sound of several songs being sung at once, the bougainvillea
and poinsettia, the country and jungle sounds at night,
everyone getting up at five and singing, and the familiarity
of it all—I know the faces of the rickshaw boys and the dogs
and the lizards, a hawk catching a field mouse, and all my
friends. After the terrible schizophrenia of Delhi, the unity
of life at Shantiniketan was a welcome thing, although
the basic fallacy of imposing the personality of a single
nineteenth-century genius upon an entire community still
causes obstacles to the process of education. There are such
marvellous people there, though, such personalities that
could never be bent to the Tagore image: Chanchal with
her marvellous Punjabi English ('I hate it when the fat in
the pan makes "Phut! Phut!"' and referring to something
she likes but can't think of the word for as 'such a rubbish
this thing'). There is a little Santhal woman who sweeps
and cooks; when I told her I was leaving she went and told
Chanchal, 'Everyone I love goes away,' and later when her
friend admired the complicated patterns that Chanchal
was knitting, the Santhal woman turned to her and said
indignantly, 'Do you think it is for nothing that they read
such small writings?'

And others: The girl who, when I tried to explain what it was to go to the movies 'Dutch Treat' instead of letting her pay for me as she wished, said, 'Oh, you mean self-help'; the Greek boy learning Sanskrit who complained about all the retroflex consonants, 'I have to put my tongue in so many places in my mouth, I'm afraid I'm going to swallow it'; and all the lovely long, long talks at night, wrapped up in blankets and shawls against the country night air, walking outside under the astonishing tropical sky.

It seems that all the best times I have had in India have been connected with singing, especially now that I know a lot of Bengali songs. Yesterday I went to Mishtuni's house for lunch; there are three sisters, Mishtu, Chiku, and Thuku (like the Marx brothers*), and they all love to sing, and to dance. They have some records of things like 'Granada' and 'La Paloma', and they insisted on being taught to rhumba, in return for which they taught me some East Bengal folk dances, usually done by bride and groom in a competition between the two houses. Gradually the afternoon degenerated into a kind of free-for-all with some rhumbas done to classical ragas, Bharatanatyam done to 'When They Begin the Beguine' [a 1938 Cole Porter song], folk dances done to the theme from *Limelight* [a 1952 Charlie Chaplin film], ballet to Rabindranath songs, and like that, until we were all too exhausted even to laugh any more, and settled down to a lunch of chicken stewed in coconut milk and a compote of papayas, tomatoes and dates.

Mishtuni teaches a class of five-year-olds English and

---

* Harpo, Groucho, Chico, and Zeppo—brothers in a comedy act from 1905 to 1949.

Bengali, and one morning when I came by and saw them under the trees in a circle around her I stopped for a minute, and they demanded a song, and then a story in English. I told them Goldilocks—'Oh,' one of them said, 'you mean *tinte bhalluk*,' which is Bengali for three bears—and I had to really ham it up for them to understand, because they don't know much English. If they missed something, they'd raise their hands and I'd say it in Bengali, and they'd laugh and laugh at the mistakes I made in Bengali and then they said poems for me in English ('Little Tommy Tupper', etc., deliciously mutilated), fighting for a chance to be next, and then poems in Bengali. One poem, about a crazy land where the kites fly boys, where you open your mouth to eat a candy and it bites you, and where in order to see clearly you have to close your eyes, was reminiscent of the Walrus and the Carpenter [from *Alice in Wonderland*] and the 'Big Rock Candy Mountain' [the American country folksong]. Then they all tried to give me their oranges and eggs and bananas, and for the next days, every time one would meet me, he'd say, 'Wendy-di Namaskar,' as you greet a teacher, and ask me if I would come back again.

When I finally did leave Shantiniketan, there were two people in my train compartment. One was an all-India football player who composed and sang original devotional songs all the five hours to Calcutta, and when we crossed the Ganges he went to the door, threw it open, and sang a song to Mother Ganges. At one point he asked me my name, and I said, 'Wendy,' and he said, 'Oh, Bindi,' and I said, 'No, Wendy,' and he said, 'Oh,' and then he said nothing for about five minutes and then suddenly said, 'I have forgotten it already. Would you say it again?' and when I did he took out a notebook and wrote down, WENDY, and that was the end of our conversation.

The other man in the compartment was a philosophy professor whose books are published by Macmillan, a grand old man of the old school, and he asked me if I knew any songs, and when I told him the ones I knew he asked me to sing them, and then he sang a lot of Sanskrit verses from the *Gita Govinda** for me, stopping every few verses to apologize, 'I'm afraid it's a bit erotic.' For a while another man came in, and *he* sang, and at the same time the football player and the philosophy professor were singing, each one to himself, but quite loud, as all Indians sing, and each one 'sculpting' the song with his hands in the Indian way, paying no attention to anyone else. Then the professor asked me why I had brought no lunch along, and I explained that I had bought some bananas but had left them by mistake at Shantiniketan, and when we stopped at the next station he jumped out and came back a few minutes later with a bunch of bananas, which he would not let me pay for, because, he said with a sad and compassionate look, 'You left your bananas at Shantiniketan.'

More strikes against Nehru: he purposely suppresses any leader that might be able to take his place, and he let Syama Prasad Mukherjee, such a leader, die in jail without a doctor to cure him;† the Congress party was responsible

---

* The 'Song of Krishna the Cowherd', about Krishna's lovemaking with his beloved Radha.

† Syama Prasad Mukherjee (1901–1953), originally part of Nehru's team, broke away, founded what was to become the Bharatiya Janata Party (BJP), and was eventually arrested; he died of a heart attack in prison under circumstances that were hotly debated.

for the great loss of Hindu life right after Partition, because they searched the Hindu houses and removed all knives etc., but not from the Muslim houses; Chanchal remembers that during Partition there was a room in the house where her uncles stayed up all night making bombs out of razor blades. And as for Gandhi, the general consensus of Punjabis and Bengalis is that if he had not been assassinated when he was, he would have ruined India in five years, by giving too many concessions to the Muslims, which he had to do because he was a Hindu and so unusually sensitive to the need to lean over backwards not to offend the Muslims. And I am really beginning to wonder what kind of a game Nehru is playing, giving money for rockets and television while everyone is starving.

A recent incident was horribly reminiscent of the Tsarina Katharina and Potemkin[*]: Nehru was to visit a village, and so all along the road he was to travel the *fronts* of the houses were painted, irrigation ditches dug (though they were completely useless until the next monsoon, by which time they would become filled in and broken down), beggars kept away, people given clean new clothes, and a great deal of money spent wastefully. The newspapers picked it up, and surely Mr Nehru must have known that Indian villages don't look like that, but for some reason he prefers to look the other way.

Last night Pradip Sen [Conchita's husband], a delightful

---

[*] An incident involving Grigory Potemkin, a lover and attendant of the Russian Empress Catherine II, gave rise to the phrase 'a Potemkin village', meaning a fake façade, much like the one in the Indian narrative about to be told.

Bengali entrepreneur, said that he wanted to bring a dancing girl to the house, and Lorraine Dimock objected because, as Pradip said, 'She won't just dance, she will show something.' Lorraine said she didn't approve of the exploitation of the female body, and Pradip said, 'We won't exploit, we will just see.' Lorraine was getting more and more resistant, and so to convince her of the advantages of the idea Pradip said, 'Don't worry, it won't cost anything. For Edward she will do it for free,' and that, of course, was the end of that, and poor Pradip couldn't understand why we were all laughing so hard.

I find that I get along best with the older generation of Indians, for my taste and view is basically classical, and I can sit around even with strangers and bemoan the passing of the good old days. Mishtuni's mother is a very beautiful woman with a magnificent body even though she is past fifty; she was a dancer, and played all the leading parts in the premiers of Tagore's dance-dramas at Shantiniketan, where Tagore himself directed them, taught them how to dance (and this was the first time that women 'of family' in India were allowed to be dancers, and it was quite a scandal), and exasperated them all by changing the entire drama the night before the performance. She had wonderful stories to tell, and so did a very old lady I met, Tagore's niece, who had been tutored by him in painting, literature, music and dancing for hours every day, and remembered every minute of it. This is the vision behind Shantiniketan—a combination of personal tutoring, education in all the arts, and a kind of saturation in Tagore's genius—but it is basically a charismatic force, in spite of its general appeal, and without Tagore it has become inconsistent and dispirited.

I met a crazy old woman ('My brain is cracked,' she said, 'and so everything I make is always a little cracked!' She had knitted a gorgeous dressing gown for her husband, using for threads the threads that she had removed from the coloured borders of hundreds of old saris) who told me how she had learned all the old stories from the Puranas and *Mahabharata* from her great-grandmother when she was young, sitting beside her while she cooked sweets and told them the meaning of Shiva. But now the families live apart; children play with their contemporaries instead of their grandparents, and since they read all day in school they don't want to listen to stories when they come home. It made me very sad, one more battle lost to the un-Indianizing forces, and it made her sad as much for the sake of the country as for her own feeling about a tradition that she was personally unable to pass on as she wished to.

My friend Ratna Jasodhara Sen Gupta was married last night, and I went to the wedding, and to her room ahead of time to help her dress. The room was filled with incense and garlands and excited girls and sighing old women and little boys all dressed up and blowing on conch shells for good luck. Ratna's friend was carefully painting the *arpana* design on Ratna's forehead and chin and hands, another friend was painting red lac on her feet, another was putting one magnificent necklace after another on her, another was weaving white flowers into her hair, and all the while Ratna was getting more and more scared. The widows dressed in plain white cotton saris would come in, tip Ratna's face up to them with a hand under her chin, smile at her, and walk away. Some stood making a peculiar noise I can only describe as ululation (I don't think I've ever had a chance to use that word before), sort of whooping and at the same time wiggling the tongue back and forth very rapidly. It's very loud and very eerie, and they do it all during the preparations and during the wedding itself, for good luck. When Ratna was finally ready, and the groom had arrived, first the groom sat on a specially painted place on the ground, and the two priests started saying verses over him. Then he changed into a new white silk dhoti and put on a special kind of pointed hat that looks very much like a wedding cake, and then he stood up and they put a silk sheet over his head. Ratna was led out, her face veiled, all dressed in red with gold, and she walked around him three times, bowing before him each time. Then she looked down, they put the sheet over her head too, and they saw each other in a mirror held below them. Then they sat beside the sacred fire, and he put his garland over her head and she put hers over his, and their hands were tied together by garlands, and flowers piled over their tied hands, and then the priest put the rupee notes that he received for the ceremony over the flowers, and blessed them, and put them in his pocket. All of this took a long time, and was very casual; people would stand around saying, 'Walk around him once more, that's right, don't sit there, sit over here, put your veil further back on your head,' and such, and while the bride and groom were sitting, their hands joined, the priest reciting verses over them, people would walk up and say, 'You look lovely, how are your studies progressing? Will you live in Calcutta now?' and it was generally jolly. The ceremony went on for about an hour, and then everyone went into the next room and ate a lovely meal served on banana leaves, leaving the bride and groom and priest sitting there. After dinner we came back in, and they were still sitting there, and finally their sari and shawl were tied together, and they walked around the fire seven times, and they were married. It was a lovely ceremony and encouraged me greatly to see how one *can* have the best of both worlds: both the bride and groom were educated at Oxford, and among the gorgeous golden saris that were given as wedding gifts there were things like books of Berthold Brecht's poetry, Van Gogh reproductions, and records of Pergolesi. For the wedding night they will sleep on a bed of *champaka* flowers (they look like white irises, and smell like Lily of the Valley), but they will use contraceptives. Just how many of this sort of best-of-both-worlds coups one can carry off without becoming schizophrenic I would not venture to say, but I would certainly give it a try.

By the way, at the wedding, and for a day preceding and following it, they play a single raga over and over again on the pipe and drum and sitar, repeating it, and one musician goes for hours and then another comes and plays. So John Cage[*] with his phrase repeated 850 times is just about as old-fashioned as they come.

---

[*] A composer (1912–1992) noted for his atonal and repetitive music. My mother knew and admired him.

29. December 20, 1963,
c/o Dimock

I've started working with Professor Hazra. He is a great scholar, and a reverent Shaivite, and he believes that he has supernatural powers, ESP and all that. He had a vision that Professor A.D. Pusalkar (also a great man in the field of Indian history) was going to have trouble with his eyes; he wrote him a cautionary letter and Pusalkar wrote back, Yes, he *was* having trouble with his eyes. Hazra showed me the letters, proudly, adding that it was no surprise to him that he could see these things, for after all his body was not in one place but everywhere—so why shouldn't he be able to see everything? He gives me tea and is of great help in the Sanskrit; I come at 7:30 in the morning, right after he finishes his yoga, when his mind is freshest. In showing me the letter he had written to Pusalkar, he said it was unusual for him to be so moved by a vision as to write a letter: 'I almost never answer my mail,' he said.

I've decided to go to Bhubaneshwar rather than Bombay. Bombay is a new, and therefore dull, city; there is nothing to see there but the caves,[*] and they are hard to get to. Moreover, there are some, although admittedly not as good, caves at Bhubaneshwar, and there are in addition the terrific temples there and at Konark. It amounts to a choice between Hindu eroticism and Buddhist serenity,[†] and I do not hesitate in that choice.

---

[*] At Elephanta. In fact, I did visit Elephanta (see 23 A. Miscellaneous travel notes, on page 171), and in 1983 I wrote, with Carmel Berkson, *The Cave of Siva at Elephanta.*

[†] From Bombay I later visited the Buddhist caves at Ajanta, as well as the great Hindu temple of Kailasanatha at nearby Ellora.

My friend Conchita is Spanish and fairly aristocratic. I began to suspect her politics once when we were singing folk songs and the song I knew as 'The Four Generals' [a song of the partisans in the Spanish Civil War] she knew as 'The Four Women'. But just the other day, she was complaining that it wasn't safe to go out in Calcutta at night alone. 'Is it safe in Spain?' I asked. 'Oh yes,' she said proudly, 'in Spain there are policemen all over.' So I guess it depends on how you look at it.

Part Seven

THE CONGRESS OF ORIENTALISTS,
AND ALI AKBAR KHAN

n this final section, punctuated by random scraps of thoughts about the whole adventure, I was already drifting away from the world of India and back into my world of Europe (the English and German Consulates) and, more particularly, academia. The 26th International Congress of Orientalists was a big deal. The first one had been held in Paris in 1873, the 25th in Moscow in 1960. For this one, the Indian government issued a special stamp that proclaimed 'XXVI International Congress of Orientalists, New Delhi' and depicted, for reasons that escape me, a statue of a buxom woman holding a representation of the yoni, or vagina, used in the worship of the Goddess. Orientalists, primarily

Government of India stamp issued to commemorate the XXVI International Congress of Orientalists, New Delhi, 1964. *Source:* Wikimedia Commons.

Sanskritists, from all over the world came to India and presented papers there, and I met many people that I knew from my years of Sanskrit study at Harvard. How I came to be invited to present a paper I cannot recall, but I was, and I did, one that I refer to in earlier letters as being about 'the humanization of the Hindu gods', a topic on which I was to publish later, though I say nothing here about its reception at the conference. I was more interested in all the people that I met there.

But the final and joyous note of this record of my time in India is very Indian indeed, the story of my passionate devotion to Indian music, more particularly the music of Ali Akbar Khan. He dominates both of the two last long letters (December 23, 1963, and February 16, 1964; the letters of February 10 and March 19, 1964, are just brief meditations), framed by reports of the Embassy parties (where my idiotic assumption that all the Germans I met were Nazis from the World War II films I used to watch is yet another embarrassment to me now) and the academic Congress in Delhi.

30. December 23, 1963,
c/o Dimock

This has been quite a week. First, there was a Christmas party at the British Consulate, and we got our good clothes out of storage, and, for a special treat, had the cook heat pans of water to wash in, and I washed with my special birthday Schiaparelli soap, and all in all I felt like a New Yorker again, staggering around in my high heels after long disuse, sticking the mascara stick carefully into my retina, puttin' on the agony.* But for all our pathetic efforts, we were country cousins at the Consulate. Boy, that's a crowd. Talk about pukka sahibs, I didn't know such people really existed. I met a woman from Trinidad, an Englishwoman, and when she was introduced to a native Trinidadian girl, a friend of mine, she said, 'You must know Collins Street in Trinidad? Well, my father is Douglas Collins. You must have heard of him. My grandfather was...' and on and on. Real ugh. But then the Christmas programme, recordings of thin, high choir-boy voices in drafty Anglican cathedrals, and someone read [Dylan Thomas's] 'A Child's Christmas in Wales', and T.S. Eliot's 'Journey of the Magi', and a really wonderful Christmas poem by John Betjeman, and then carols, and mulled wine, and a lovely tree. As always, the music touched the spots that I can hide from everything else in India but familiar music, and I remembered going carolling through the Boston hospitals with the Harvard Glee Club, and the overheated smell of the wards after walking through the snow, and the time we sang the Messiah in Symphony Hall and the way I felt when, after singing for two hours, we all rose for the Hallelujah Chorus, and I missed it terribly.

At this party I met the German consul, and he invited me to the German Consulate party the next night, and I went. Well, of course it's a truism that the expatriates and colonizers from a country are always the scum—the pukka sahibs at the British Consul would be despised by the English as much as they are by the Indians here. And

* A line from a 1957 song by Lonnie Donegan, 'Puttin' on the Style'.

then too, national characteristics are always exaggerated abroad—the Americans, present company included, find new depths of Americanism in themselves, and seem almost caricatures. But when you get the scum and the exaggeratedly nationalist of Germans you know who you've got, and Donnerwetter,* but that's who was at the German consulate. It really made my flesh crawl, and I began to perspire freely. I'd never actually *met* one before, and here was a whole room full of them right in the middle of Calcutta. I felt as if I'd stepped into some sort of time machine and suddenly landed in the middle of Gestapo headquarters in a movie. The blond curly-haired and blue-eyed lads in their dark blue suits, standing with their heels together; the consul himself with watery pale blue eyes with no eyelashes, and an oily, thick face; the vice consul with pale skin and a wet, red mouth; even a man with a squeaky voice and very, very thick round glasses; several men with 'game legs' and it was all I could do to keep from asking, 'A war injury?'; the clipped, sibilant speech—the whole thing was so fantastic that I was positively hypnotized by it, until suddenly I became nauseous and quickly left. But I'll never forget it.

Well, then a wonderful thing happened to me. I met Ali Akbar Khan, India's greatest sarod player. He is to the sarod what Ravi Shankar is to the sitar, but Indians consider Ali Akbar a far greater musician, and a much nicer man. (Ravi Shankar doesn't associate with Indians much now, and one Indian friend of mine pointed out the similarity

---

* Literally, 'Thunderweather', a German expression of astonishment and anger.

between this snobbery and that of Duke Ellington, which I was surprised that he knew about.) As a matter of fact, Ali Akbar's father [Ustad Alauddin Khan, 1862–1972] is the greatest musician of them all (he is 101 years old now and still practises for fifteen hours a day); he taught Ravi Shankar, and Ravi Shankar married Ali Akbar's sister (rather like the Gandhis and Nehrus). I asked Ali Akbar how it was that Ravi Shankar was so much more famous in America while he (Ali Akbar) was so much more famous in India. 'Ravi Shankar spends 10,000 rupees a month on publicity,' he said. 'I spent the money on whiskey and I am more happier.' He gets tremendous pay for a concert, but he explained that it was necessary because, being a Muslim, he has four wives to support; his father, however, only recognizes the first wife, and says 'the rest are kept, not married', which has caused great family strife. But Ali Akbar lives with none of them now, but has a very nice room in the Great Eastern Hotel (the Carlyle* of Calcutta); when I asked him why, he said, 'When I play lots of concerts I want to be peaceful, and at home they are always making me to eat.' So, during the concert season, December and January, he moves into a hotel. There were two beds in the room, one made up for him, and the other for his sarod. 'He must be peaceful too,' says Ali Akbar. To see him, you'd never think him an artist, and I guess in this respect he's India's answer to Isaac Stern, the fat little boy from Brooklyn. Ali Akbar is short and fat, leans back and his stomach sticks out; his face is like a cross between

---

* A particularly elegant New York City hotel, where President Kennedy used to stay.

Akim Tamiroff and Rocky Marciano, fleshy, jolly, with a bald head and a fringe of hair around his ears like a monk. When we went to the house where he was to play that night, he carried his sarod in a case shaped somewhat like a violin case and looked for the life of him like a mobster carrying a machine gun. When I first met him, he came to his hotel room door with little puffs of shaving cream all over his face, and when he learned that I had just cut my hand a little, he immediately insisted on putting iodine on it himself, and blowing on it to keep it from stinging, all the time with the shaving cream still on his face.

Then we went to the house where he was to play, to celebrate the food-taking ceremony for a friend's six-month-old daughter. He sat cross-legged on a Persian rug, wearing white pyjamas and a little grey vest, and tuned his sarod. The sarod is a far richer and more versatile instrument than the sitar; the sitar is like Chianti, but the sarod is like champagne. While the sitar is made of a large gourd with a wooden fingerboard, the sarod is carved of wood, with a goat-skin stretched over the bowl, and a long metal fingerboard with the metal strings stretched close to the board, and no frets. You slide a sarod rather than finger it, and if you're Ali Akbar, you can do the most marvellous things with it. Try to imagine Segovia, Oistrakh, Dave Brubeck, and Earl Scruggs all rolled into one, and that's just the beginning. He played for eight hours, all night, and the whole thing was improvisation on a raga. At first he played by himself, without the tabla, and he played slowly and sadly, keeping a steady rhythm with the strumming hand, but somehow managing to produce a legato melody by sliding along the strings. It was like wind on water, or an animal crying out, and sometimes like the ocean, or like keening. There was no question of understanding complex rhythmic patterns or note systems: it was pure emotion, immediately intelligible and moving. I had wondered, when I first heard of it, how anyone could listen to music all night, but I understand now. Though the rhythm continues steadily, there is no pattern of long duration in the melody, but the momentary patterns of an inspiration. He sits with his head down, strumming, with his fingering hand relaxed on his leg, and suddenly he'll reach out and caress the instrument for a few notes, and then let his hand drop back, and then reach out and dart up and down in a terrifically intricate run, sounding like birds fighting, and again the hand relaxes, and it's like a conversation, each spurt entirely different, and clearly marked with an emotion, even subtle emotions like disgust and impatience, as well as the more forceful moments of grief or love or anger. And you simply hold your breath during the steady strumming, wondering what he will say to you next. Sometimes he would pluck a string hard once, and then without striking it again he'd play an entire tune by sliding up and down on it in slow and then suddenly quick and then slow motions, until the sound died out. Sometimes he'd pluck it and then let it suddenly fall, and it sounded to me the way I'd always imagined the sound of the breaking string in the distance in *The Cherry Orchard.** There was infinite variety in it, and he played like this,

---

* A play by Anton Chekhov, which ends with the sounds of a string snapping and an axe cutting down a cherry tree.

unaccompanied, for about three hours. And all the time, in the room spread with white cloths on the floor, with everyone sitting cross-legged, people kept moving in the rhythm, but there was not a sound, except, when sometimes he'd play an unbearably beautiful melody, or in the faster part later on play simply more and more and more until you couldn't believe it, when he finished the run there would be a gasp, or a cry of approval almost like an *olé*, and he would smile at us, and then look down again and wait for a new mood, sometimes moving his fingers over the strings without actually touching them as he waited to pluck a new rhythm or melody out of the air. The room grew warm and he took off his vest and mopped his bald head from time to time with his left hand, still keeping up the strumming with his right. The strings would go out of tune, and he'd tighten them, still plucking out a melody on the string, tightening it in short spurts so that he played a melody on the string he was tightening all the time he was tightening it.

After a while there was a break, we ate dinner, and then the second part began, with the tabla. It was marvellous fun; they kept the same basic rhythm, but the tabla would play variations in the rhythm while the sarod played variations on the raga, sometimes in the same rhythmic variation as the tabla, sometimes different. They would 'joke and fight', as Ali Akbar later described it; the tabla can play melodies by striking different parts of the two drums, and of course the sarod can play complex rhythms by the strum, and they would imitate one another, and pick up one another's variations, and sometimes they would look at each other and smile and finish off a long run with a loud, fast, perfectly together coda, and everyone would laugh with delight. It was like a Dixieland jam session in spirit, but with an Elizabethan elegance, and an Indian sweetness. Sometimes the sarod would be very mournful but the tabla very excited beneath it, and sometimes the tabla would beat out a steady, funereal rhythm while the sarod went all crazy with little runs, and sometimes they would play in the same mood. It was altogether the most wonderful music I have ever heard.

When it was over, we went back to Ali Akbar's room for breakfast, and he played a tape of a trio between himself, Julian Bream on the lute, and Larry Adler on the harmonica, all improvising, and it was simply out of this world. And then, wonder of all wonders, when he saw my enthusiasm he asked if I would like to learn, and he said he would give me some lessons ('I practised for eighteen hours a day for twenty years, but if you do an hour a day that will be alright too') and would get a sarod for me (he can get marvellous ones for little money, because then the sarod maker can say that he makes Ali Akbar's sarod, which is of course tremendous prestige) and my first lesson will be on Christmas day. Tonight he and Ravi Shankar are playing an all-night duet, and I am to come as Ali Akbar's guest.

There was a hiatus in my letters home during the month of January, when my mother, Rita Doniger, came to India and we travelled together. And, before she arrived, I wrote a series of letters filled with nothing but tedious travel arrangements, which I have left out. (I revisit Rita's time in India in the Postscript to this book.) Only one anecdote popped up in a footnote in a letter dated January 10, 1964: 'I have the supreme Mysterious East item. I cabled [my fiancé]: "Gird your loins", which, after processing by the inimitable Indian wireless operator, emerged as, "Gird your lions".'

∾

31. February 10, 1964,
c/o Dimock

Aminah ran away with Shyamkumar, the bearer.

I have come to terms with my emotional reactions to India, helped by your fresh eyes to see things I have learned to take for granted, supposedly for my own good but perhaps really false to my true Weltanschauung and therefore in the long run exacerbating—but I have come to terms, and am content to love India for its culture and hate it for its inhumanity, as one comes to terms with a man one loves even though he may not be perfect. India is still the one I love, but not to the desecration of my own ideals of the way the Good Life should be lived and I believe it can be lived in the West with an eclectic world of Indian thoughts and things.

I just found out that it takes the train to Dhaka, 150 miles from Calcutta, twenty-eight hours to make the trip.

They're renaming all the streets here in a burst of nationalism, throwing out the British; but then you get instances of Wellington Street now being named Acharya

Jagadish Chandra Bose Road, so of course everyone still calls it Wellington Street, and you can't find anything.

32. February 16, 1964,
c/o Dimock

I finally got around to typing up my notes from the past month or so and here they are.

The International Congress of Orientalists, that met in Delhi last month, was a great delight to one who fears the eventual and characterless merging of all individual cultures. Not even in the UN have I ever seen national characteristics so much in evidence, because of course all UN people are diplomats, driving in big cars and drinking and generally living the same sort of life, but scholars don't have enough money to shed their nationalities, and anyway they are just Menschen by nature. In Delhi at the Congress everyone seemed a caricature of his culture, and it was quite a circus. The Americans talked through their noses and wallowed in their jargon and called everybody by his first name and told one another what *they* did for their diarrhoea. The Russians were red-faced and hirsute, and turned every seminar and convocation into an occasion to Spread The Word: they read papers on such topics as 'Anti-Capitalist Literature in 19th Century India', 'Indian Miniatures in the Leningrad Collection', 'Problems of Economic Cooperation of USSR and India', etc., and gave speeches containing such gems as 'The friendship between Soviet scholars and the young nations of the East is based on the principles formulated by the great Lenin. Following these principles, the Soviet state has been waging an irreconcilable struggle against colonialism, against all forms of race and national discrimination, social and economic oppression, as has been stressed many a time by the indefatigable champion of peace, Nikita Khrushchev. In our work we must not be influenced by the feelings of chauvinism and narrow nationalism cultivated in some places...', etc., etc. The Germans used words like Zeitgeistvereingungsliteraturkunstgeschichte and read papers proving, by the use of astronomical data, that the Aryans came to India from the Arctic Circle in 15,000 BC. The French chattered like birds, got terribly excited and angry at everybody, and read papers relating the *Kama Sutra* to the erotic sculptures of Tibetan temples.

And the Indians! They really stole the show, reading papers proving that the Vedas were written by God (after reading this paper, when the author came to the customary question period, he announced, inscrutably of course, 'There will be no questions. Om.'), proving that the Theory of Relativity will have to be revised in the light of Jain metaphysics, and showing that the principles of caste are based on a necessary and natural division existing in all physical forms including the atom and the lever; and they conversed in Sanskrit, waggling their heads and making private jokes—how private can you get?—and waving emaciated fingers. It was great fun, and the best thing was that people I know were assembled there from the most various worlds, making it a most unlikely and constantly unsettling reunion, like the dinner party at the end of *Alice in Wonderland*, or the great ball at the end of *Mary Poppins* or the parade at the end of the circus. There was Gordon Wasson,[*] just flown in from the East where he is working on mushroom madness in New Guinea; and Harvard people, and Shantiniketan people, and people whose books I'd read, and even people from Great Neck, for chrissake!

I made the interesting discovery that all Sanskritists are heavy drinkers; they came trooping off the planes with manuscripts under one arm and bottles under the other; W. Norman Brown, the Grand Old Man of American Indologists, and a serious drinker himself, said that he thought this tendency could be traced back to a historical misconception from the pioneer work in Indology in the nineteenth century, when it was thought that Soma[†] was a form of alcohol: 'Now, of course, we know it wasn't alcohol but some kind of drug, but whatever it was, it couldn't be as good as bourbon.'

Delhi is a hotbed of syncretism, women twisting in saris, Muslim women in purdah carrying transistor radios, and mourners using Zippo lighters to ignite the funeral pyres. Old Rudyard[‡] knew what he was talking about; this East and the American West, at least, can't meet, and the attempts to do it are pretty sickening. But I've come to see that this does not necessarily mean a choice between medieval Indian charm and poverty or modern American

---

[*] R. Gordon Wasson was a mycologist with whom, in 1968, I wrote my first published essay, in his book, *Soma: Divine Mushroom of Immortality*.

[†] That the Soma plant was a drug, indeed a hallucinogenic mushroom, rather than a source of alcohol was the argument of the book that Wasson and I were working on.

[‡] Rudyard Kipling, author of the lines, 'Oh, East is East and West is West, and never the twain shall meet.'

vulgarity and prosperity. In architecture, for instance, one can have the best of both worlds, as in Madras, where sturdy and practical modern houses are being built, but not in the Californian style that is so ridiculous in Bombay or the Corbusier impracticality of Chandigarh (which now gives the impression of Arp sculptures* used as poles for clotheslines). The Madras buildings keep the thatched roof (more practical, cheap and attractive than tile) and latticed windows, remaining purely Indian and still made of preshrunk† concrete. So it can be done. But it isn't done often enough, because of the absence of true pride in things Indian.

The latest development is that with all the anti-Pakistan propaganda, the government is making a serious and insidious effort to wipe out all traces of Persian culture in India. Libraries are no longer stocked with Persian books, Persian paintings aren't displayed in the museums, and now the courts are trying to declare national laws purposely opposed to the laws of Islam. This is the kind of thing that sickens me at heart.

And it makes me appreciate all the more a man like Jamini Roy, India's most famous and, I think, best modern painter. His works are, as they say, 'deceptively simple', stylized from the elements of Indian folk painting, and terribly strong. Jamini is a very old man now, and still fighting the good fight. He paints his paintings as an offering, because he must, and then says that if he went

---

* Jean Arp (1886–1966) created highly abstract sculptures.

† I think I must have meant pre-fabricated.

down to the river and floated them away to the ocean, like
the image of the Goddess that is immersed in the Ganges
on the day of Durga Puja, they would still be fulfilled. He
paints what is basic to all men, and his paintings have a
medieval Everyman look to them, and this all the more
because they are purely Indian; he feels that one must first
be truly oneself, be, say, a Bengali, and one must be truly
Bengali before he can be a citizen of the world, and he is.
He once said that he can paint the whole world right from
his studio because he has it all within him (like Picasso's
reply when asked why he didn't use a model), and colours
enter his eyes, everyone's eyes alike, like tunes entering
the ear; all the world, hearing church bells, bows the
head; hearing a military march, the head comes up. He
feels that painting should be like that, and his is. And in a
way I felt that his idea has much of its roots in the Hindu
concept of caste, in the way that it divides people; an
Indian painter has more in common with a British painter
than he has with an Indian businessman; I find that I have
more immediate rapport with the musicians and dancers
I've met here than with most of the people at home. It's
not that people aren't divided, but that the divisions are
temperamental and occupational, not national. And with
all this, it's ironic that Jamini's paintings are held in little
esteem in India outside his own circle; his themes are too
familiar to the Indians, embarrassing them, and they feel
that it can't be 'art', though the way in which he uses the
themes is certainly art. The American GIs, of all people,
discovered his work during the war, and he became famous
in Europe, while still neglected by the Indian people whose

spirit he is trying so hard to preserve, to reveal to them, to help them value.

Night after night I've been going to the concerts of Ravi Shankar and Ali Akbar Khan, very beautiful and moving music. The two men are strikingly different, though they are good friends, brothers-in-law, and embrace warmly backstage after each concert. Ravi Shankar is very fiery and temperamental, showing off, wearing fancy shirts, making the sitar look as difficult as possible, speaking French to his admiring retinue. Ali Akbar sits like a Buddha, half asleep all the time, and strokes the sarod casually as if he were stroking a sleeping cat. Before each concert a man comes out and puts a garland over the head of each of them, and they take them off before they begin to play; Ravi Shankar drapes his dramatically over the edge of the platform, and Ali Akbar drops his into a little pile behind him, and therein lies the essential showmanship of the two of them. Ali Akbar is teaching me to play the sarod because, as he puts it, 'My dream is that someday Indian music should be available all over the world, like Chinese food.' Before the concert, Ravi Shankar had his palm read, while Ali Akbar tuned in his transistor radio to the cricket commentary (even though another station was broadcasting a tape of a concert he had played in Delhi); as he sat cross-legged, people trooped in to pay homage to the guru by touching his feet and laying the 'dust' from his lotus feet on their heads. But as he is very fat, and had his legs tucked under him, they had a hard time finding his feet, grovelling with their hands under his knees, and he didn't pay any attention to them at all, let alone move. He asked me if I could sing

Indian music, and I said no, it sounded too queer to me, and he asked me how, and I showed him, and he said, 'It sounds as if you're rewinding your throat.' And it did.

I am now in possession of a very beautiful sarod, upon which I have already learned to play 'Greensleeves' for you, Daddy (you always forget the name, but 'Greensleeves' is the one you like).

33. March 9, 1964, chez Dimock

I have decided to go to Kathmandu instead of Darjeeling (it is deeper in the mountains and the weather is clear there, whereas this time of year is cloudy and misty in Darjeeling), and I'm going on Wednesday. With the usual Doniger luck I unknowingly picked the best day of the whole year to go there; when I told Professor Hazra that I was going, he told me that Thursday is Shivaratri, the Night of Shiva, which is the most holy night of the Shaivas, and the most sacred place for its celebration is the Pashupatinath temple in the mountains of Kathmandu, where thousands of pilgrims come for the Shivaratri festival, and I'll be there. In the daytime, I'll play in the mountains, and then I'll come back to Calcutta on the 15th, in time to catch my breath and get on the plane on the 21st.

I told you that I was playing 'Greensleeves' on the sarod, didn't I? Well, last night Ali Akbar played a concert, and I saw him before it, and he asked me how the sarod was coming along (he's been out of town for a week), and I admitted to playing 'Greensleeves', and he laughed. And then at the concert he played one kind of a theme known as Ragamala, a 'Garland of Ragas', with lots of different themes woven in, and right smack in the middle he played something that sounded like an Indian version of 'Greensleeves', and the more I listened the more I realized that it *was* 'Greensleeves', with Indian touches, and it sounded like a real raga, and Ali Akbar was grinning like the Cheshire cat.[*]

This may be the last letter before I see you, unless of course you write something that 'requrs an ansr', as Wol[†] would say. Until then, I'll just save it to tell you at Idlewild on the 22nd.

---

[*] Yet another character in *Alice in Wonderland.*

[†] A character in *Winnie-the-Pooh.*

Postscript

M y final letter, on March 9, 1964, includes two statements about the future: 'I've decided to go to Kathmandu...on Wednesday' and 'I'll just save it to tell you at Idlewild on the 22nd'. (I was still calling the New York Airport Idlewild, though it had been renamed the John F. Kennedy International Airport in December 1963, after Kennedy's assassination.) I was a bit delayed in meeting my parents at Idlewild on March 22, and it was Chanchal's fault. She had put into my hands, right before I boarded the plane, a bag with a dozen ripe Punjabi mangoes; she knew how I loved mangoes, and of course insisted that the best ones came from Punjab. They were my main nourishment on the long flight back to the States, but I still had six of them left when I deplaned in New York. To my horror, the airport officials refused to let me take them out of the customs shed with my luggage. Unwilling to throw out six fabulous Punjabi mangoes, I sat down right there, took out my knife (in those days before

Pan Am 103, we were able to take knives onto planes) and ate one mango after another, while everyone else took their luggage and left, the customs officials looked at their watches, and my parents waited anxiously for me on the other side of the barrier. When I had eaten the last mango, I went home.

Ali Akbar and I remained friends over the years, and when I lived in Berkeley (1975–78), I often visited him over the bridge in San Rafael, where he had founded a music school in 1967, and where he died in 2009. I had intended to continue playing the sarod in America, and indeed I brought my sarod home with me, on my lap on the plane all the way back, at some considerable inconvenience. But just a month after my return from India, I was in a serious automobile accident, which smashed in my skull and shattered my left knee and broke all the bones in my right arm. I was in hospital for three months and then went home by ambulance to recuperate for several more months; my right arm was in a cast for over a year. And after that long hiatus, somehow I never played the sarod again, though I always kept it with me, at Harvard, in Oxford, in Berkeley, and now in Chicago as I write this.

There are two serious lacunae in the letters that I feel the need to address here. First: Since my mother was with me on my travels in January and February there was no point in writing letters to her about that. Second: On the flight to Kathmandu in March, I met Penelope Betjeman, a relationship that changed my life. (This lucky encounter with Penelope in a plane at the end of my time in India perfectly balanced my similar meeting with Ed Dimock

in a plane at the start.) And since I flew home right after
the trip to Kathmandu, there was apparently no time to
write to anyone about that. There is therefore no record
of the trip I took all around India with my mother, nor of
the meeting with Penelope. I did write about both of these
women elsewhere,* but as for my adventures with them
in India, the letters are silent. Let me say just a few words
about both of those trips, and both of those women, now.

My mother flew into Madras on January 18, 1964.
Norman Brown, who was staying in Madras at that time,
graciously drove me to the airport and waited with me
there for her. Years later, at a memorial service that I held
for my mother in Chicago after her death in 1991, Norman
still recalled her vividly as she descended from the plane in
Madras, carrying a New York salami in her hand luggage,
the one thing she felt I most needed in India. From Madras,
Rita and I went to Mahabalipuram, where we stayed in a
lovely thatched bungalow right on the shore, from which
we wandered about admiring the great free-standing
statues, and even climbing on the statue of Shiva's great
bull Nandi. Every night there was a delicious meal served
al fresco from a little open kiosk on the beach; we carried
our food away on great palm leaves and sat down to eat
it on the sand by the ocean. We also travelled up into the
hills above Madras to see a Kathakali performance of the
Mahabharata in a village.

We flew to Calcutta on January 27, where we stayed
with the Dimocks and Rita met Jamini Roy and bought

---

* See the chapters on Rita Doniger in *The Donigers of Great Neck* and on
Penelope Betjeman in *Winged Stallions and Wicked Mares.*

Rita Doniger at the Sun Temple, Konark.

several paintings from him, that she hung in places of honour in the house in Great Neck. From there we travelled to Bhubaneshwar, where we stayed at the State Guest House and visited Konark and Puri. We swam in the ocean in Puri; the surf was strong, but we were well protected by lifeguards wearing elaborate white hats that looked like wedding cakes. After a brief return to Calcutta, we spent a week (February 10–16) in Benares.

My mother had grown up in Vienna but had lived in America ever since she married my father in 1938; she had been back to Europe only once since then, touring with me and my father in the summer of 1958, and had never been to Asia. Yet now, at the age of fifty-three, she travelled alone to India and then, despite the early rumbles of the Vietnam war, went on by herself to visit Angkor Wat,

From the Kathakali performance at a village
in the hills near Madras.

as she had always dreamed of doing, visiting her brother
in Guam before returning to New York. Travelling with
me in India, she was so adventurous that I was the one
who had to try, always in vain, to keep her from getting
into trouble, reversing the usual parental roles. She, not
I, was the one who distinguished herself by handling a
large python around her neck in Benares. And when we
went up into the hills above Madras to see the village
performance of the *Mahabharata*, and they offered us food
of such unknown provenance that I would have boiled it
for several hours before putting a single bite in my mouth,
and I frowned and gave her a meaningful look and firmly
shook my head, she went blithely ahead and ate it all and
didn't even have the courtesy to get sick afterwards. When
we stayed at a seaside hotel in Puri, she laughed like a

schoolgirl at the sight of cockroaches the size of lobsters scampering across our room at night. She was an awfully good sport. And in 1991, when she was dying, she told me that her visit to me in India was the single most wonderful experience of her whole life.

Rita with a snake around her neck, Benares.

Penelope Chetwode Betjeman, who was to become a second mother to me (and godmother to my son), was sitting in the seat beside mine when I boarded my flight to Kathmandu. We instantly became friends and remained friends until she died, in 1986. In Kathmandu, I was staying in some sort of Dak Bungalow, but Penelope was staying in the palace with the Maharaja. (Her father, Field Marshall Sir Philip Chetwode, had been Commander in Chief of the

British forces in India from 1928 to 1935, and Penelope had grown up there.) On one occasion, she invited me to dine at the palace; after dinner, the Maharaja showed us around, and I noticed, among the signed, framed photographs of the crowned heads of Europe, one of Adolf Hitler, which gave me a bit of a start. On a different occasion, Penelope,

who had ridden horses since she was six months old, rode in a small race around the miniscule track on the palace grounds; disdaining to use the whip as the other jockeys did, she allowed them all to lap her twice, on two full circuits, and as she finally came into the home stretch she patted her pony's neck, 'to demonstrate kindness to animals', she later explained to me. Penelope was a devout Catholic convert, and as I was, at that time, seriously contemplating becoming a Catholic myself, we spent a lot of time together at a local convent. This was the beginning of a beautiful friendship.

With a nun at the local convent in Kathmandu.

I never again spent more than a month at a time in India, though I made many short visits, sometimes on research grants for particular projects, sometimes lecturing to groups from the University of Chicago, always to visit friends. On one of those trips, in the mid 1980s, I took my son Mike with me. But I never went back to Calcutta or Shantiniketan.

In 2009, I spoke at the Jaipur Literary Festival about my new book, *The Hindus: An Alternative History*, and I was planning to return to India in 2010, to accept an award for that book. My little brother Tony, now all grown up, was going to accompany me, with his wife, and we planned to continue on to tour India together. But there was a bit of legal trouble about *The Hindus*, and it might have been dangerous for me to return to India. My brother and sister-in-law went without me (circumspectly travelling under her name, rather than use the name of Doniger), and they met my brave publisher, whom I, alas, have still never met in person. I doubt that I will ever see Shantiniketan again.

Bibliography of Works by Wendy Doniger
mentioned in notes to the letters

'Part II: The Post-Vedic History of the Soma Plant'. In *Soma: Divine Mushroom of Immortality*, by R. Gordon Wasson, pp. 95–147; also served as Vedic consultant and co-author. New York: Harcourt Brace, 1968. Reprint, Harcourt Brace Jovanovich, 1971; paperback, 1973.

Asceticism and Eroticism in the Mythology of Siva. Oxford University Press, 1973; OUP India, 1975. Paperback, retitled as *Siva: The Erotic Ascetic* (New York: Galaxy, 1981).

The Origins of Evil in Hindu Mythology. Berkeley: University of California, 1976; Delhi: Motilal Banarsidass, 1976; paperback, 1980. 411 pp. Italian translation, *Le Origini del male nella mitologia indu* (Milan: Adelphi Edizioni, 2002).

Women, Androgynes, and Other Mythical Beasts. Chicago: University of Chicago Press, 1980; Delhi: Motilal Banarsidass, 1980; paperback, 1982.

The Rig Veda: An Anthology, 108 Hymns Translated from the Sanskrit. Harmondsworth: Penguin Classics, 1981.

The Cave of Siva at Elephanta. Photographs by Carmel Berkson, text by Wendy Doniger O'Flaherty, Carmel Berkson, and George Michell. Princeton: Princeton University Press, 1983.

Dreams, Illusion, and Other Realities. Chicago: University of Chicago Press, 1984; reprinted, paperback, 1985; Delhi: Motilal Banarsidass, 1987.

Splitting the Difference: Gender and Myth in Ancient Greece and India. The 1996 Jordan Lectures. Chicago and London: University of London Press and University of Chicago Press, 1999; Indian edition, Delhi: Oxford University Press, 2000; paperback, 2002; Italian edition, Milan: Adelphi Edizioni, 2009.

The Woman Who Pretended to Be Who She Was. New York: Oxford University Press, 2005.

The Lady of the Jewel Necklace and The Lady Who Shows Her Love. Harsha's *Priyadarshika* and *Ratnavali.* Clay Sanskrit Series. New York: New York University Press, JJC Foundation, 2006; Indian edition, with an introduction by Anita Desai; Kindle edition, 2017.

The Hindus: An Alternative History. New York: Penguin Press, 2009; Delhi: Penguin Books, 2010; Oxford: Oxford University Press, 2010. Second edition, New Delhi: Speaking Tiger, 2015; Kindle edition, 2017.

The Ring of Truth, and Other Myths of Sex and Jewelry. New York: Oxford University Press, 2017. Indian edition, retitled as *The Ring of Truth: Myths of Sex and Jewelry* (New Delhi: Speaking Tiger, 2017). Italian edition, titled *L'anello della verita* (Milan: Adelphi Edizione, 2019).

The Donigers of Great Neck: A Mythologized Memoir. The 2015 Mandel Lectures at Brandeis. Waltham, MA: University Press of New England/Brandeis University Press, 2019.

Winged Stallions and Wicked Mares: Horses in Indian Myth and History. Charlottesville and London: University of Virginia Press, 2021; New Delhi: Speaking Tiger, 2021.

The Dream Narrative: Dreams of God and Mortals in Classical Hinduism. New Delhi: Speaking Tiger, 2022.

'Wars Within the Womb, in Classical Hindu Mythology'. In *Gemini and the Sacred: Twins and Twinship in Religion and Mythology,* edited by Kimberley Patton. London: Bloomsbury, forthcoming, 2022.